PRAISE FOR *CONVERSATIONS WITH LINCOLN*

"Bravo to Gordon Leidner for opening a window to little known encounters between Abraham Lincoln and everyday Americans. These conversations will further elevate our knowledge and appreciation of a leader for all seasons."

—Ronald C. White Jr., author of *A. Lincoln: A Biography* and fellow at the Huntington Library

"Leidner has provided an anecdotal biography of Lincoln that shows how much of his character went out with his words. From the famous to the unknown, observers recount their interactions with America's most iconic president, surprised that the nation's chief executive not only listened to so many, but most importantly, he cared. These 'conversations with Lincoln' bear witness to Lincoln's generous wit, greatness of soul, and philanthropic mindset."

—Lucas Morel, editor of *Lincoln and Liberty* and professor of ethics and politics at Washington and Lee University

"Have you ever wondered what it would have been like to meet Abraham Lincoln? Now you can know! In this wonderful volume, Gordon Leidner has brought together some of the most poignant firsthand accounts from men and women who actually met Lincoln. Covering from his young adulthood in Illinois in the 1830s up through his last full day of life in 1865, we encounter Lincoln as a humble, selfless man who cared about the lives of his friends, neighbors, and constituents. This is a book that every Lincoln lover should read."

—Jonathan W. White, author of *Lincoln on Law, Leadership and Life*

"A marvelous collection of little-known accounts by people who met Lincoln. Their stories are often heartrending, and some will bring tears to the reader's eyes."

—William C. Harris, professor emeritus of history from North Carolina State University and author of *Lincoln and the Border States*

"This impressive collection presents vivid, detailed accounts of Abraham Lincoln from all phases of his life. Here we encounter more evidence of his generosity, his humanity, and his wisdom."

—Joan E. Cashin, professor of history at Ohio State University and author of *First Lady of the Confederacy*

CONVERSATIONS WITH LINCOLN

LITTLE-KNOWN STORIES FROM THOSE WHO MET AMERICA'S 16TH PRESIDENT

GORDON LEIDNER

CUMBERLAND HOUSE™

Published by Cumberland House, an imprint of Sourcebooks, Inc.
P.O. Box 4410, Naperville, Illinois 60567-4410
(630) 961-3900
Fax: (630) 961-2168
www.sourcebooks.com

Library of Congress Cataloging-in-Publication Data

Names: Leidner, Gordon, author.
Title: Conversations with Lincoln : little-known stories from those who met
    America's 16th president / Gordon Leidner.
Description: Naperville, Illinois : Cumberland House, an imprint of
    Sourcebooks, Inc., 2016. | Includes bibliographical references and index.
Identifiers: LCCN 2015049409 (hardcover : alk. paper)
Subjects: LCSH: Lincoln, Abraham, 1809-1865--Miscellanea. |
    Presidents--United States--Biography--Miscellanea.
Classification: LCC E457.909 .L46 2016 | DDC 973.7092--dc23 LC record available at
http://lccn.loc.gov/2015049409

Printed and bound in the United States of America.
WOZ 10 9 8 7 6 5 4 3 2 1

To my beautiful daughters:
Melony, Sarah, and Cate. Great conversationalists.

CONTENTS

PREFACE

ABRAHAM LINCOLN WAS ONE of America's most accessible presidents. In spite of the daily trials of the Civil War, throughout his entire four years at the White House, he kept the executive mansion open to visitors. Practically anyone who was willing to come to the White House and wait for hours in the hallways or waiting rooms received a chance to talk to the leader of the Great Republic.

During sunlight hours on visiting days, guards at the front door rarely interfered with a visitor's access. Most people simply walked up to the second floor of the White House, spoke briefly to an attendant, and took a seat in the waiting room. Cabinet members, officers of high rank, and other notable persons such as members of Congress usually had priority, but not always. If the door attendant discerned your business would be of particular interest to the president, you might be moved ahead of the "important personages." But, given the president's busy schedule, people frequently waited for hours or even days. Many gave up before they had their opportunity to talk to him.

Those fortunate enough to attain access to the president's office frequently found him alone, seated in an armchair, reading or writing. Without ceremony, he would look up from his papers, rise slowly to his great height, and, with a surprisingly warm smile, say, "I am glad to meet you" or "What can I do for you?"

Unless the visitor's business was conducted quickly, they were usually asked to sit down and "tell him all about it." To their surprise—no matter how trivial the subject—the president was an avid listener. He looked them in the eye and asked pertinent questions. If someone else could better attend to their business, Lincoln would pull out his ever-present pencil and write directions on a piece of paper or ring a bell to summon a secretary, whom he would ask to investigate the matter for him. If the visitor's request was something that only the president could address, such as an appeal for a pardon or the release of a soldier from duty, his "legal" mind took over, and he carefully read any pertinent papers before responding.

Frequently, the visitor's requests were granted. President Lincoln was an excellent judge of character, and when he felt it was safe, he took people at their word. When the situation demanded, he asked an attendant to do additional research and sent the visitor away, telling them to "come back tomorrow." If he decided their request could not be granted, he told his visitor immediately. Lincoln had earned a reputation for honesty when he was a young man, and now that he was president, he wasn't about to change.

He had soft spots. The requests for mercy from women, particularly widows, soldiers' wives, or mothers with children, would rarely be refused. Any request for a soldier's pardon from a death sentence was a priority with him. He searched for any excuse to spare their lives—much to the frustration of the secretary of war, who flatly told him that his frequent pardons undermined military discipline. Once, when reproached for his refusal to allow a soldier to be shot for cowardice, he stood by his decision and stated, "I am just as God made me, and cannot change."

The White House was not the only place where Lincoln encountered the public. People approached him virtually everywhere. Sometimes the president could be seen on the street, pencil in hand, writing out a response to a passerby's request. He could often be found in one of the capital's twenty-five hospitals with a melancholy look in his eye, shaking hands and offering words of encouragement to the wounded. Since soldiers were among his favorite people to visit, he was often in the camps around the capital, reviewing troops or informally chatting with men and officers.

Abraham Lincoln genuinely loved people. Having grown up in a poor family with (as he once said) "no wealthy or popular relations to recommend" him, he sympathized with visitors, saying he knew how they felt.

Many of the stories herein were recorded by people who personally knew Lincoln in the nineteenth century but are not usually mentioned in contemporary Lincoln biographies. For example, India Frances Brown, a Confederate soldier's wife, broke down in tears while pleading for her husband's life and was quickly comforted by the president when he took her baby into his arms. The former slave Nancy Bushrod forced her way past White House guards in a desperate attempt to see Lincoln on the last day of his life and asked him to help her and her children. Countless soldiers in hospital beds, whose names are lost to history, wept unashamedly when they received a warm handshake or word of kindness from the president who had come to thank them for their sacrifice.

It's all in here. The melancholy appearance, the informal greeting, the warm smile and handshake, the earnest desire to grant a favor, save a life, or tell a funny story—these were all Abraham Lincoln. So open the door—the president will see you now.

GORDON LEIDNER

INTRODUCTION
A GIRL'S REQUEST

A DETERMINED YOUNG GIRL *named Hannah Slater decided to pay a visit to President Lincoln one morning in early 1863. The previous year, her father had been severely wounded in the war while a captain in a New Jersey regiment, and he was now in danger of losing his desk job at the Chain Bridge commissary department due to the disfavor of a superior officer. Hannah had suggested that her father visit the president himself to plead his case, but, feeling that his troubles were too trivial to warrant an audience with the president, he refused. She thought about it all night and then resolved that, the very next day, she would take the case to the president herself, without her father's knowledge.*

Bright and early the next morning I was up and dressed in my best Sunday frock, my hair carefully braided, with my prettiest hair-ribbons and hat; and leaving word that I had gone out to do an errand, I started for the White House.

The streets seemed quiet, and I wondered why.

It was late in May, and the sun was high, so it did not occur to me that it was still early. I had quite a walk to the White House and when I reached there, no one seemed to be around. I went up through the great portico to the front door and rang the bell. After what seemed to me a long wait, a tall doorkeeper opened the door, and, looking much surprised to see me standing there, said bruskly,

"What do you want?"

"If you please, sir, I should like to see the President."

He looked at me in amazement. "Well," he said, "you certainly are making an early call. Don't you know the doors aren't open until nine o'clock?"

"No, sir," I replied, "I am a stranger here, and I don't know anything about your rules and regulations, and I haven't any idea what time it is."

"Well," he answered, "the President isn't even up yet, and anyway he's not receiving visitors these days. For two or three weeks he has not seen anyone except on urgent business."

"Oh!" I exclaimed, "My business is important! I *must* see him. My father is an Army officer and in trouble, and I must tell the President about it."

"Well," he replied, "if the President could see

you, it would not be before eleven o'clock, and it's not seven yet. You would have a long wait, should he see you at all, which I think is doubtful. Do you live far from here?"

"Yes sir, I do."

"Well, which would you rather do, go home and come back, wait outdoors, or—would you like to come in?"

"If you please," I said, "I would like to come in."

"Very well," he decided, "you may go up to the second floor into the reception room; but remember, I don't believe you can see the President."

I went up as he directed and looked about the room, and out of the windows, enjoying especially the views out over the lovely grounds. By and by I began to hear stirrings above me and I decided the President must be getting up. After a long time I went across the hall and looked out of the front windows and saw crowds of people coming from every direction. At last the doors were opened, and by ten o'clock the rooms upstairs and down were packed. It was a distinguished-looking company; all the Army and Navy officers with gilt braid and buttons, and foreign diplomats in full regalia, and fashionably dressed women. And how anxious they all were to see the President! I heard one lady say:

"I have been coming here every day for three weeks hoping to see Mr. Lincoln, and have not succeeded in having an interview with him yet."

Another replied: "I have been coming every day for weeks without being able to see him. I want my son transferred from one hospital to another, and the authorities won't do it. I know if I could see President Lincoln for five minutes he would grant my request."

So one after another I heard these people telling of their daily disappointment, and I began to feel pretty hopeless. I was only a little girl; this was my first visit, and I knew I could never get up sufficient courage to come again if I failed this time. I had just about decided I had better go, when I saw the tall doorkeeper come in, looking all about for some one. There were Generals and Admirals, and all sorts of important-looking personages, and I supposed he was trying to find one of them. But suddenly I saw him beckoning to me. I looked at him questioningly, and he nodded. I went to him and he whispered,

"You may see the President now."

How can I describe my feelings? It seemed too

good to be true, and yet, in spite of my happiness, I was so frightened I could scarcely move. I mustered up courage, however, to follow him. He opened a door and pushed me in: and there I was—all alone with the President.

Mr. Lincoln was sitting in an armchair in the farthest corner of the room. Seeing my timidity, he rose, and beckoning in a friendly way said: "Come this way, Sis; come this way."

His voice was so kind and gentle that all my fright left me immediately. He came in great strides to meet me, and taking me by the hand, welcomed me most cordially.

"And did you wish to see me?" he inquired.

"Yes, Mr. President," I replied, "My father is in trouble and I have come to tell you about it."

"Does your father know you have come?"

"Oh, no, Mr. President. He would not have allowed me to come if he had known anything about it. I wanted him to come, himself, to see you, but he said you were too burdened for him to trouble you, and he would not come. I stayed awake all last night thinking about his trouble and decided I would come myself. So before he was up, I slipped out of the house without his knowledge."

A kindly smile lighted President Lincoln's face and he said: "Come sit down and tell me all about it."

His sympathy made me feel at ease, and I told him all the story in detail. When I was telling him of Father's being wounded at the Battle of Fredericksburg and of the necessity of the amputation of his leg, and of his and Mother's sufferings, he interrupted me.

"So your father was wounded at Fredericksburg?" he said.

"Yes, Mr. President," I answered.

He threw his head back on the chair, and as he clasped his hands before him and closed his eyes, a look of agony passed over his face. With a groan, he said: "Oh, what a terrible slaughter that was! Those dreadful days! Shall I ever forget them? No, never, never." Then recovering himself, he said: "Go on, my child, go on."

So I went on and told him all about our leaving our old home; of Father's appointment to Chain Bridge and of the indignity he had suffered; of his anxiety concerning the welfare of his big family; and how, only the day before, the Division Commander had seemed to threaten his removal.

When I was all through, the President said:

"My child, every day I am obliged to listen to many stories such as yours. How am I to know what you have told me is true?"

"I'm sure I don't know, Mr. President," I replied, "unless you are willing to take my word for it."

"That's just what I'm going to do," he said as he patted me on the shoulder. "I will thoroughly investigate this affair," and taking a notebook from his pocket, he made a memorandum of what I had told him. Then closing the book, he said: "Now, my child, you go home and tell your father not to worry any more about this. I will look into the matter myself, and I will see to it personally that no further injustice is done him. He can rest assured that he will either be retained in his present position or have a better one. It will come out all right, I can promise you."

Grasping his hand in both of mine, all I could say was: "Thank you so much, Mr. President."

"That's all right, my child, all right." And then rising he bade me good-bye with all the graciousness he would have shown some notable woman, and bowed me out.

I stood for a moment fairly dazed. How unbelievably marvelous it all seemed, and what a wonderful man our President was!

I fairly walked on air all the way home, and I could hardly wait for Father's return that evening. At last I saw him coming on his crutches, care-worn and worried. Mother met him at the door with the usual question,

"Well, Father, how have things gone today?"

"No better, Mother," he answered sadly.

Then I could restrain myself no longer and cried out, "It's all right, Father! Everything is going to be all right!"

"What's all right, child? What do you mean?"

"Well," I said, so happy that I could scarcely talk coherently, "I went to the White House today and saw the President and told him all about your trouble—"

"You went to see the President!" he interrupted, "What on earth did you do that for? I never dreamed of your doing such a thing! The President never heard of me. He doesn't know a thing about me. Why should he be troubled with my affairs?"

"Well," I replied, "you refused to go to him because you said you would not bother him with your troubles; so I went to him, myself. I told him all about it, and I have a message for you from Mr. Lincoln. He told me to tell you not to worry one bit more, that he would investigate the matter personally and you should either keep your present position or have a better one."

The expression on my father's face was a study. Bewilderment, amazement, incredulity, and joy were all mingled.

"Did I ever!" he cried. "Bless your heart!"

Gathering me in his arms he held me close, struggling to keep back the tears that were threatening.

The President kept his word. He did just what he said he would. In a few days, when the General made his next visit to the station, he was as courteous as he could be to Father.

"Good morning, Captain," he said, and came to Father's desk to transact business with him for the first time.

And after that, in all their relations, there was never the slightest shadow of unpleasantness.

I never saw the President to speak to him again. Within two years he was dead, and our hearts grieved as if he had been one of our own. But down through the years I have had this memory of the big-hearted, sympathetic man, burdened by affairs of state, beset by hundreds of people, as he sat patiently, unhurriedly, listening to the story of a little girl.

CHAPTER ONE
BACK IN ILLINOIS

———◆———

TO GAIN A FULLER understanding of President Abraham Lincoln in 1861, we must go back thirty years and envision a young man who was drifting silently alone down central Illinois's Sangamon River. This youth was twenty-two years old, poorly clad, and appeared to possess little more than a melancholy demeanor and a tall, muscular frame. All of his worldly belongings were in a battered old canoe. He had recently left the family farm and struck out on his own, looking forward to beginning a new chapter in life. His destination was the pioneer village of New Salem, Illinois, where he had been promised a job as store clerk by a local businessman.

The story of Abraham Lincoln's life up to the day he arrived in New Salem was fairly typical of young men in nineteenth-century rural America. He had been "raised to farm work" and acquired all the job skills he needed to survive on the prairie. Being a poor farmer's son, his formal education had totaled less than a year, but this was hardly an impediment to an aspiring village store clerk. Nevertheless, this drifter on the river was different—quite different from most men his age—in that he had a "peculiar ambition" to be "truly esteemed of my fellow men."

He was different in other ways too. Physically, he was a study in contrast. His immediate appearance was that of a dull laborer or farm hand, but when engaged in conversation, his entire demeanor changed. People were struck with his bright eye, his wit, and his sense of humor. Additionally, he had been blessed with an exceptional memory and an unquenchable desire to learn. He had an inherent sense of justice, accompanied by a genuine interest in helping those in need. Consequently, he had a positive impact on many lives, and for these reasons, people liked Abraham Lincoln. They remembered him.

Lincoln quickly made friends in New Salem. His unique ability to compose and tell funny stories always kept his listeners laughing. He was a conscientious store clerk who treated customers fairly, and it was while working as a store clerk that Lincoln earned the sobriquet "Honest Abe." Older men and women appreciated his willingness to help others and do favors for people in the community. The young men of the neighborhood admired his ability to outrun, outjump, and outwrestle nearly all of them. Young women found his awkward attempts to communicate with them amusing.

Children adored him because he was always willing to tell a story or play a game.

While in New Salem, Lincoln worked at several jobs besides store clerk: boatman, mill hand, postmaster, volunteer soldier, election clerk, and surveyor. Although these jobs paid very little, they proved invaluable in honing Lincoln's people skills. As a postmaster, he became acquainted with virtually everyone in the community. As a volunteer militia officer in the Black Hawk War, he learned something of leadership and sacrifice. As a surveyor, he learned how to resolve disputes between neighbors.

When Lincoln was a child, he had always been interested in learning and was often in trouble with his father for taking time out from farm work to read. Now, as an adult in New Salem, he was able to read to his heart's content and borrowed books on a wide range of subjects, including grammar, history, mathematics, literature (especially Shakespeare), astronomy, and law. He was also interested in improving his ability at public speaking and joined a local debating club.

People in New Salem noticed Lincoln's efforts at self-improvement, and several of them encouraged him to run for the lower house of the Illinois State Legislature—which he did in 1832. Although he lost this election, he resolved to continue studying law and try again for the legislature.

Lincoln was self-conscious about his meager education and impoverishment and wanted to help others better themselves. Consequently, he joined the recently formed Whig Party, which he believed stood for economic and social progress, and ran again for the state legislature in 1834.

On his second attempt, he won the election. Lincoln journeyed south to take up temporary residence in the State Capitol of Vandalia and began his immersion in the legislative process as a member of the Whig constituency. After a productive term as a freshman legislator, he was reelected to another term in 1836. Thanks to his diligent studies of law, he was admitted to the Illinois bar and became the junior partner in fellow legislator John Todd Stuart's law practice. Although Lincoln's true love was politics, the state legislature only met for a few short months during the year, and the pay was paltry. Consequently, Lincoln's principal residence remained New Salem, and his primary vocation was attorney-at-law.

The job of attorney suited Lincoln well. He used his humor and story-telling skills to his advantage and developed into a talented speaker. Lincoln was, according to several of his peers, "the strongest jury lawyer we ever had in Illinois." His reputation as an honest lawyer was well deserved, and Circuit Judge David Davis would later attest to the fact that a dishonest case was poorly represented by

Lincoln. As an attorney, he had plenty of opportunities to help people in need. To the chagrin of the other lawyers, he charged clients less than the customary fees when he felt people were in financial difficulty and charged nothing at all in particularly needy cases.

Lincoln was fond of New Salem, but the population of the village was dwindling, because people were moving away to more promising communities in the region. So in 1837, Lincoln decided to move to nearby Springfield, whose thirteen hundred inhabitants made it the second largest city in the state after Chicago. Upon arrival, he moved in with a man who would become one of his closest lifelong friends, Joshua F. Speed.

Lincoln won reelection to the legislature again in 1838, and thanks largely to his efforts in that governmental body, the capital of Illinois moved from Vandalia to Springfield the following year. Lincoln's legal business continued to prosper, and in 1839, he not only practiced law in Springfield, but also on the Eighth Judicial Circuit in surrounding counties. Lincoln's star was on the rise, both professionally and socially, and in that same year, he met John Todd Stuart's cousin, the sophisticated Mary Todd from Kentucky. A romantic relationship followed, and they became engaged in 1840, the same year Lincoln won his fourth term in the legislature.

After a stormy courtship, Lincoln and Mary Todd married in 1842 with a ring Lincoln gave to Mary inscribed with the sentiment, "Love is eternal." Their first son, Robert, was born in 1843, and a second son, Eddie, was born in 1846—the year Lincoln was elected to the U.S. House of Representatives.

Lincoln moved to Washington, DC, and he began his two-year term in Congress. Although he did his best to represent his constituents, his term was rather uneventful except for his effort to introduce a bill that would end slavery in the District of Columbia. Lincoln had "always hated slavery," and although bills to end slavery in the District had been proposed by others before, they had all failed. Lincoln decided to write one that he hoped would receive greater bipartisan support. Although he wrote a draft of the bill and worked diligently to line up support, he soon discovered that he did not have enough political clout to guarantee its passage. Consequently, he did not formally introduce it to the House of Representatives for a vote.

In early 1849, after his single term in Congress, Lincoln decided to return to Illinois, put his political career on hold, and pursue law more diligently. While his law career became increasingly successful, the Lincolns were grieved by the death of their three-year-old son Eddie in

1850. This event had a significant impact on Lincoln, and although he had avoided church for many years, he started to develop a friendship with James Smith, the pastor of the First Presbyterian Church in Springfield. Mary joined the church, and Lincoln began to attend occasionally. He and Mary were soon cheered by the news that they were expecting another child. Willie was born in December of 1850, and another son, Tad, was born in 1853.

Even though Lincoln had stopped pursuing political office, he remained attentive to the hottest political topic of the time: slavery. He believed that slavery was a blight on the principles of equality expressed in the Declaration of Independence and declaimed his belief that the founding fathers had intended for the evil institution to die out. He became increasingly outraged with the Democratic Party's indifference to the spread of slavery into the new territories west of the Mississippi River. He advocated the preclusion of slavery in the western territories with the hope that most of the newly formed states west of the Mississippi would become free states, causing the balance of power in Congress to shift away from the South and allowing the nation to eventually eliminate slavery.

In 1854, one of Illinois's senators, Democrat Stephen A. Douglas, pushed the Kansas-Nebraska Act through Congress, allowing the territories west of the Mississippi to decide for themselves whether slavery could spread there. Lincoln was incensed over this development and decided it was time to reenter the political arena in order to add his voice to those who condemned slavery.

An Illinois Senate seat was up for grabs in 1854, and Lincoln wanted it. He ran as a Whig candidate for that office but lost the race because the Democrats held a majority in the state legislature.[1] In 1858, incumbent Senator Stephen A. Douglas's term was up for renewal, so Lincoln ran for the office again, this time as a Republican.

Lincoln had switched to the Republican Party, which had just been founded in 1854, because its antislavery beliefs effectively defied the proslavery Democratic Party. But Lincoln and the Republican Party of Illinois were significantly challenged, because the Democratic Party was very strong in Illinois, where the majority of the state's population was highly prejudiced against African Americans.

Lincoln and Douglas gained national attention as they stumped the state while debating the issue of slavery. Lincoln pleaded with Americans to return to the ideals of equality expressed in the Declaration of Independence. Although he

---

1   Prior to 1913, U.S. Senators were chosen by their respective state legislatures, rather than the direct vote of the people. It was not until the ratification of the 17th amendment in 1913 that senators were elected by the direct vote of the people.

avoided pushing for complete social equality between the races at this time, he nevertheless took the first step toward that end by declaring slavery a moral evil that should die. Douglas, in the meantime, demeaned African Americans and indifferently claimed that slavery was a local issue that should be decided by the states or territories.

Lincoln suffered defeat again, losing the Senate race to Douglas. However, his oratory skills during the debates launched him into the national limelight, and he became one of the nation's leading voices for the abolition of slavery. He was nominated as the Republican Party's presidential candidate in 1860 and defeated Stephen A. Douglas and two other candidates in the national presidential election in November of that year. The southern slave owners proclaimed that as president, Lincoln would force an end to slavery, so after the election, southern states began declaring their independence. Abraham Lincoln, the agreeable prairie lawyer and storyteller from Illinois, would soon, as president of the United States, hold the nation's fate in his hands.

The following stories illustrate Lincoln's growth in Illinois from an ungainly, twenty-two-year-old store clerk to one of the most influential men in the country. Although Lincoln became a powerful leader, he still retained his good nature, moral ascendancy, and the high esteem of all who knew him.

———◆———

LAWYER HENRY C. WHITNEY, in his book Life on the Circuit with Lincoln, *presents a picture of the impoverished, awkwardly clad young Lincoln in New Salem in the early 1830s. The account clearly shows that not everyone who knew Lincoln at that time believed he was going to move up in the world.*

When [Lincoln] first ran for the Legislature he presented this appearance: He wore a blue jeans coat, claw hammer style, short in both the sleeves, and in the tail:—in fact, it was so short in the tail he could not sit on it: homespun linen trousers, a straw hat and "stogy" boots.

Of course this was putting the best foot forward, but ordinarily, in his youthful days, when not posing as a candidate, he was dressed thus:

"He wore flax and tow-linen trousers—about three inches too short: one suspender; no vest or waistcoat. He wore a calico warmus, such as he had in the Black Hawk War: coarse brogans, color of the native hide; blue yarn stockings and straw hat, minus a band and turned up behind."

Judge Matheny informs me that when Lincoln

first ran for the Legislature it was regarded as a joke; the boys wanted some fun: he was so uncouth and awkward, and so illy dressed, that his candidacy afforded a pleasant diversion for them, but it was not expected that it would go any further. It was found, however, during the canvass, that Lincoln knew what he was about and that he had running qualities: so Matheny told him he was sowing seeds of success: and that next year he would win. And he did.

ROBERT L. WILSON WAS a lawyer and fellow legislator whom twenty-five-year-old Lincoln befriended while living in New Salem. In 1834, Lincoln was still working various odd jobs, including store clerk and surveyor. In the following description, Wilson introduces the lanky, good-natured young man who had recently studied a surveying book so that he might become the county's deputy surveyor.

Mr. Lincoln had the monopoly of finding the lines, and when any dispute arose among the settlers, his compass and chain always settled the matter satisfactorily. He was a good woodsman, at home in the dense forest. He was a genial, fun-loving young man, always the center of the circle where ever he was. Every one knew him, and he knew every one. His stories and fun were fresh and sparkling, never tinctured with malevolence; he never told a story about an acquaintance with a view to hurt or hold up to ridicule, but purely for fun. The victim always enjoyed it as much as any one else, esteeming it rather a compliment, than a sarcasm, being entirely destitute of malice.

Mr. Lincoln at this time, was about twenty-four or five years old—six feet four inches high in his stockings, some stoop shouldered; his legs were long, feet large; arms long, longer than (those of) any man I ever knew. When standing straight and letting his arms fall down his sides, the points of his fingers would touch a point lower on his legs, nearly three inches, than was usual with other persons. I was present when a number of persons measured the lengths of their arms on their legs, as here stated, with that result; his arms were unusually long for his height, and the droop of his shoulders also produced that result. His hands were large and bony, caused no doubt by hard labor when young; he was a good chopper; the axe then in use was a great clumsy tool, usually made by the country blacksmith, weighing about six pounds, the handle being round and straight, which made it very difficult to hold when chopping, requiring a grip as strong as was necessary to wield a blacksmith's sledge hammer. This and running barefoot when young among stones, and stumps, accounts for his large hands and feet.

His eyes were a bluish brown, his face was long and very angular; when at ease (there was) nothing in his appearance marked or striking, but when enlivened in conversation or engaged in telling, or hearing some mirth-inspiring story, his countenance would brighten up, the expression would light up, not in a flash, but rapidly the muscles of his face would begin to contract, several wrinkles would diverge from the inner corners of his eyes, and extend down and diagonally across his nose; his eyes would sparkle, all terminating in an unrestrained laugh in which every one present, willing or unwilling, was compelled to take part.

ALTHOUGH SOME OF "THE boys" of New Salem saw Lincoln's candidacy for the legislature as a joke, there were more prominent citizens who took Lincoln quite seriously. One such citizen was Dr. Gershom Jayne, a physician, whose story was relayed by his son, Dr. William Jayne, in the early 1900s.

I [William] first met Mr. Lincoln in 1836, more than sixty years ago. He was then residing at New Salem, where he was Deputy surveyor under Thomas Neale, and also Postmaster at that village. He had then served one term in the Legislature of Illinois and was a candidate for a seat in the Legislature at the election to be held in the following August. At that time there was something about this ungainly and poorly clothed young man that foretold to an observing person a bright future in public and political life.

At this meeting we had a dinner on that day at the Rutledge Tavern in New Salem; and afterwards during our journey along the road from New Salem to Huron, where Mr. Ninian W. Edwards, who was in our party on that drive, and my father, had a country store. Mr. Lincoln became the subject of what we then called the "talk" between Mr. Edwards and my father. Some time afterwards Mr. Edwards became a brother-in-law of Mr. Lincoln. What was said about Lincoln during that conversation I now remember as distinctly and vividly as if it had occurred only on yesterday. Among other things my father said to Mr. Edwards, "Edwards, that young man, Lincoln, will some day be Governor of Illinois." I was then only a lad ten years of age and thought my father was a very hopeful prophet. I had seen at Springfield two Governors of Illinois, Ninian Edwards of Belleville and Joseph Duncan of Jacksonville. These two Governors often came to Springfield and were always well dressed. Each came in his carriage, with fine horses and colored drivers. Mr. Lincoln up to this time had only been a captain of Volunteers in the Blackhawk Indian War and had served one term as a member of the Legislature. He did not then look to me like a prospective Governor. I then had in my mind's eye those stately gentlemen, Edwards and Duncan, but it seems that my father's foresight was much better than his son's, for in a little over twenty years this poorly clad and unknown young man was the chosen ruler of a nation numbering fifty millions of people, and was commander-in-chief of more than a million men—of a more effective and potential army than Caesar or Napoleon had ever marshalled in battle array.

In April 1837, when Lincoln was twenty-eight years old, he moved from New Salem to Springfield. By this time, he had given up his jobs as surveyor, village postmaster, and store clerk and focused

on the law and politics. The population of Springfield was grow-
ing rapidly, and Lincoln, as an up-and-coming lawyer, decided to
take up residence there. Lincoln's first interview after his arrival in
Springfield was with store owner Joshua F. Speed, who details the
circumstances of their meeting.

He had ridden into town...on a borrowed horse,
with no earthly property save a pair of saddle-
bags containing a few clothes. I was a merchant at
Springfield, and kept a large country store, embrac-
ing dry goods, groceries, hardware, books, medi-
cines, bed-clothes, mattresses, in fact, everything
that the country needed. Lincoln came into the store
with his saddle-bags on his arm, and said he wanted
to buy the furniture for a single bed. The mattresses,
blankets, sheets, coverlid, and pillow, according to
the figures made by me, would cost seventeen dollars. He said that was perhaps cheap enough, but
small as the sum was he was unable to pay it. But
if I would credit him till Christmas, and his experi-
ment as a lawyer was a success, he would pay then,
saying, in the saddest tone, "If I fail in this, I do not
know that I can ever pay you."[2] As I looked up at

---

2   Lincoln had already incurred a debt of over a thousand dollars as a
     result of the failure of one of his businesses in New Salem. It would
     take him over fifteen years to pay this off.

him I thought then, and think now, that I never saw a sadder face. I said to him, "You seem to be so much pained at contracting so small a debt, I think I can suggest a plan by which you can avoid the debt and at the same time attain your end. I have a large room with a double bed up-stairs, which you are very welcome to share with me." "Where is your room?" said he. "Up-stairs," said I, pointing to a pair of winding stairs which led from the store to my room. He took his saddle-bags on his arm, went up stairs, set them down on the floor, and came down with the most changed countenance. Beaming with pleasure, he exclaimed, "Well, Speed, I'm moved!"

LINCOLN'S FONDNESS FOR CHILDREN was well documented by friends and neighbors in Springfield. For instance, a neighborhood boy named Fred T. Dubois recalled how he and his friends liked to stretch a line of string across the sidewalk and knock off Lincoln's stovepipe hat as he walked home from the office. Then, knowing Lincoln would take the ambush in good humor, they would "raise a mighty yell, rush out from our hiding places, grab hold of him wherever we could find a place and shout for joy." Lincoln's business associate Stephen T. Logan could also attest to this fondness for young people, having returned to his house one day to find Lincoln absorbed in a game of marbles on the floor with his [Logan's] children.[3] *One of the older boys of the neighborhood, William Thompson, recalled this testimony to Lincoln's friendship with the boys on the street:*

I lived half a block from Mr. Lincoln's…and visited at the house, but more frequently I met Mr. Lincoln on the street as I went to and from school… [Mr. Lincoln] had endeared himself to all of us by reason of the interest he took in us. When one of us spoke to him as he was walking along in his absorbed manner he would stop and acknowledge the greeting pleasantly. If the boy was small Mr. Lincoln would often take him up in his arms and talk to him. If the boy was larger Mr. Lincoln would shake hands and talk with him. It he didn't recall the face, he would ask the name, and if he recognized it he would say, "Oh, yes; I remember you." If the boy was a comparative stranger Mr. Lincoln would treat him so pleasantly that the boy always wanted to speak to Mr. Lincoln after that whenever he met him.

But besides showing interest in us, Mr. Lincoln was exceedingly popular with the boys in the

---

3   Lincoln had arrived early at the Logan residence and was waiting for his friend to come home. See Roberts, *Lincoln in Illinois*, 48–49.

neighborhood because of the fishing trips of the Sangamon river he took with us. He owned a bay horse, which was called a "shaved-tail" horse. He had a "calash," as the roomy vehicle was known. Into the calash Mr. Lincoln would put all of the boys of the neighborhood who could crowd in, and drive out to the Sangamon. We carried our lunches and spent the whole day. After we were pretty well tired tramping about we spread out the lunches. Mr. Lincoln sat down with us. When we had eaten he told us stories and entertained us with his funny comments. No boy who had accompanied Mr. Lincoln on one of these fishing trips willingly missed another.

———◆———

GEORGE T. M. DAVIS, editor of an Alton, Illinois, newspaper, recorded the following story of a visit he had with Lincoln and two of his sons. Davis thought that the way Lincoln dealt with his sons in this little incident was a testament to the fair-minded, honest character of Abraham Lincoln.

I made a visit on business one summer to Springfield, where Mr. Lincoln resided. While I was standing on the sidewalk, on the shady side of the hotel where

I was stopping, Mr. Lincoln came along with his youngest pet boy, Tad, who was holding on to the tip of the tail of father's frock coat. We drew up chairs in the shade and at once engaged in talking politics. Tad changed his position by taking refuge between his father's knees, and remained there a silent listener during our conversation. In a short time [Lincoln's son] Bob, who was considerably older than Tad, came along, and, noticing us, also stopped and joined our circle.[4] In a side conversation that ensued between the two brothers, the purport of which I had not noticed, something was said that induced their father to pause for a moment in his talk with me, and, turning to the boys, he exclaimed:

"Tad, show Mr. Davis the knife I bought you yesterday," and, turning to me, he added, "It's the first knife Tad ever had, and it's a big thing for him." Tad hesitating and making no reply, his father asked. "You haven't lost your knife, have you?"

"No, but I ain't got any," the boy said.

"What has become of it?" inquired Mr. Lincoln in his quizzical and usual smiling, pleasant way. There was another momentary pause on the part of Tad, when he replied to his father, in the fullness of

---

4   Bob was ten years older than Tad.

his childish simplicity, and the truthfulness which was a prominent element of his birthright:

"Bob told me if he was me, he'd swap my knife for candy." At this Mr. Lincoln gave one of his good-natured laughs, and turning to Bob—who by this time bore somewhat the semblance of slight embarrassment—but without the slightest change in either his merry tone or manner, asked:

"Bob, how much did you pay for that candy?" Bob naming the price, his father said to him, "Why, Tad's knife cost three bits (37 and a half cents); do you think you made a fair trade with Tad?"

Bob, in a prompt and manly tone, which I shall never forget, answered his father, "No, sir," and taking the knife out of his pocket, said "Here, Tad, is your knife," which Tad, with evident delight, took back, but without a word of comment. Their father, however, said to the eldest:

"I guess, Bob, that's about right on your part, and now, Tad, as you've got your knife, you must give back to Bob the candy he gave you for the knife."

Tad exclaimed, "I can't, 'cause I ate up all the candy Bob give me, and I ain't got no money to buy it."

"Oh!" said Mr. Lincoln, "what will you do then? Bob must have his candy back to make things square between you." Tad was evidently in a quandary, and was at a loss how to get out of it, but his father, after waiting a few moments, and without making the slightest comment, handed Tad a bit (12 and a half cents).

Tad looked at it with a good deal of satisfaction and shrieked out in his boyish glee: "Come on, Bob, I'll get your candy back for you."

Both the father and I joined in a hearty laugh, and as the boys started off Mr. Lincoln called out to them: "Boys, I reckon that's about right between you. Bob, do you take Tad right home as soon as he has paid you the candy."

Such was the sense and conviction of duty, justice, honor, integrity and truthfulness of Abraham Lincoln.

LINCOLN'S REPUTATION AS AN honest lawyer and politician had made him one of the most popular men in Illinois, and his debates with Douglas had also brought him national fame. But this rise in notoriety did not diminish Lincoln's friendly manner with people.

The German-American politician and future Civil War general Carl Schurz recalled meeting Lincoln on a train the day before the sixth debate with Stephen A. Douglas at Quincy in October 1858. In the following story, the twenty-nine-year-old Schurz was impressed with the now-famous Abraham Lincoln's familiar, cordial ways with everybody.

All at once, after the train had left a way station, I observed a great commotion among my fellow passengers, many of whom jumped from their seats and pressed eagerly around a tall man who had just entered the car. They addressed him in the most familiar style: "Hello, Abe! How are you?" and so on. And he responded in the same manner: "Good evening, Ben! How are you, Joe? Glad to see you, Dick!" and there was much laughter at some the things he said, which, in the confusion of voices, I could not understand. "Why," exclaimed my companion, the committeeman, "there's Lincoln himself!" He pressed through the crowd and introduced me to Abraham Lincoln, whom I then saw for the first time.

I must confess that I was somewhat startled by his appearance. There he stood, overtopping by several inches all those surrounding him. Although measuring something over six feet myself, I had, standing quite near to him, to throw my head backward in order to look into his eyes. That swarthy face with its strong features, its deep furrows, and its benignant, melancholy eyes, is now familiar to every American by numberless pictures. It may be said that the whole civilized world knows and loves it. At that time it was clean-shaven, and looked even more haggard and careworn than later when it was framed in whiskers.

On his head he wore a somewhat battered "stove-pipe" hat. His neck emerged, long and sinewy, from a white collar turned down over a thin black necktie. His lank, ungainly body was clad in a rusty black dress coat with sleeves that should have been longer; but his arms appeared so long that the sleeves of a "store" coat could hardly be expected to cover them all the way down to the wrists. His black trousers, too, permitted a very full view of his large feet. On his left arm he carried a gray woolen shawl, which evidently served him for an overcoat in chilly weather. His left hand held a cotton umbrella of the bulging kind, and also a black satchel that bore the marks of long and hard usage. His right he had kept free for handshaking, of which there was no end until everybody in the car seemed to be satisfied. I had seen, in Washington and in the West, several public men of rough appearance; but none whose looks seemed quite so uncouth, not so say grotesque, as Lincoln's.

He received me with an off-hand cordiality, like an old acquaintance, having been informed of what I was doing in the campaign, and we sat down together. In a somewhat high-pitched but pleasant voice he began to talk to me, telling me much about the points he and Douglas had made in the debates at different places, and about those he intended to make at Quincy on the morrow.

When, in a tone of perfect ingenuousness, he asked me—a young beginner in politics—what I thought about this and that, I should have felt myself very much honored by his confidence, had he permitted me to regard him as a great man. But he talked in so simple and familiar a strain, and his manner and homely phrase were so absolutely free from any semblance of self-consciousness or pretension to superiority, that I soon felt as if I had known him all my life and we had long been close friends. He interspersed our conversation with all sorts of quaint stories, each of which had a witty point applicable to the subject in hand, and not seldom concluding an argument in such a manner that nothing more was to be said. He seemed to enjoy his own jests in a childlike way, for his unusually sad-looking eyes would kindle with a merry twinkle, and he himself led in the laughter; and his laugh was so genuine, hearty, and contagious that nobody could fail to join in it.

———◆———

LAWYER JAMES O. CUNNINGHAM recalled a special event held at the Urbana, Illinois, fair grounds on September 24, 1858. Lincoln had been invited to make a political speech to a crowd, and a dinner had been arranged for everyone. They had set up long tables outdoors, and Lincoln was placed at a seat of honor at the head table.

He took the seat prepared for him, while the long tables were assailed by his followers, and began eating his dinner. Looking around, he saw an old woman standing not far away looking intently at him. He at once recognized her as a waiter and dish-washer at the hotel in Urbana, whom everybody knew as "Granny." He said to her, "Why, Granny, have you no place? You must have some dinner. Here, take my place." The old lady answered, "No, Mr. Lincoln, I just wanted to see you. I don't want any dinner." In spite of her protestations, Lincoln arose from his seat at the head of the table and compelled her to take his place and have her dinner, while he took his turkey leg and biscuit and, seating himself at the foot of a nearby tree, ate his dinner, apparently with the greatest satisfaction; meanwhile Granny Hutchinson filled the place at the head of the table and ate her dinner as he had insisted she should do.

This episode was characteristic of Lincoln. It required no unbending of assumed dignity, for, while he was at all times manly, he put on no airs of dignity. Instinctively he sympathized with the lowly wherever he met them, and the look of the lowly woman, standing aloof from those who were being fed, with no one to speak to her, appealed to his sense of right and he placed her in his preferred place, he taking for himself the lowly attitude. It was that same instinct that made him the friend of the black slave, and the emancipator of the race.

ON OCTOBER 15, 1858, Alton resident Henry Guest McPike saw Lincoln and Stephen A. Douglas in the seventh and last debate. McPike, like many others in the audience, was spellbound by Lincoln's moral arguments against slavery.

When Lincoln was introduced he gained the immediate attention of his audience. He threw into his voice and gestures an animation that bound the audience with a spell. When he touched on the slavery feature of his address, it seemed to me there came an eloquence born of the earnestness of a heart convinced of the sinfulness—the injustice and the brutality of the institution of slavery, which made him a changed man… His long arms rose and fell and swayed in air in gestures which became to the audience under his spell models of grace and beauty. His tones rang out clear, and his resonant voice proclaimed with profound conviction the doom of slavery or the doom of the nation. "A house divided against itself cannot stand," said he, "and this nation must be all free or all slave," suiting his words to those of the Christ when he denounced sin and said that sin and unrighteousness could not exist with righteousness in the heart of the same individual. He argued that the principles of slavery and freedom could not exist in the nation side by side… I forgot the ungainly form and homely face and seemed to see the great heart of Lincoln beating in its horror at the infamy of the institution against which he inveighed. Wild and long continued cheering from Republican throats punctuated the points of Lincoln, while the Democrats stood silently or glumly listening to his discourse...

The Alton debate was a great one—some asserting it was the greatest of the seven... It made such an impression on my mind that today the tones of Lincoln are still vibrating in my ears, and it stirred my heart as nothing else did and made me a greater foe of the institution of slavery.

DR. NEWTON BATEMAN, PRESIDENT of Knox College, had been an admirer of Lincoln since he first met him in 1842. Bateman had many serious conversations with Lincoln about slavery and democratic government, and in recalling those, he stated that Lincoln was "the saddest man I ever knew." But he also knew that Lincoln had a powerful way with words, and Dr. Bateman fondly recalled a conversation the future president had in Springfield with a wary southern visitor.

One day there entered Mr. Lincoln's room a tall Southerner, a Colonel Somebody from Mississippi, whose eye's hard glitter spoke supercilious distrust and whose stiff bearing betokened suppressed hostility. It was beautiful, says Dr. Bateman, to see the cold flash of the Southerner's dark eye yield to a warmer glow, and

President-Elect Abraham Lincoln: 1861

the haughty constraint melt into frank good-nature, under the influence of Lincoln's words of simple earnestness and unaffected cordiality. They got so far in half an hour that Lincoln could say, in his hearty way: "Colonel, how tall are you?" "Well, taller than you, Mr. Lincoln," replied the Mississippian. "You are mistaken there," retorted Mr. Lincoln. "Dr. Bateman, will you measure us?" "You will have to permit me to stand on a chair for that," responded the Doctor. So a big book was adjusted above the head of each, and pencil marks made at the respective points of contact with the white wall. Lincoln's altitude, as thus indicated, was a quarter-inch above that of the Colonel. "I knew it," said Lincoln. "They raise tall men down in Mississippi, but you go home and tell your folks that *Old Abe tops you a little*." The Colonel went away much mollified and impressed. "My God!" said he to Dr. Bateman, as he went out. "There's going to be war; but could my people know what I have learned within the last hour, there need be no war."

CHAPTER TWO

OBSERVING THE PRESIDENT

———◆———

ABRAHAM LINCOLN WAS SWORN in as president of the United States on March 4, 1861. Four years earlier, his name was hardly known outside of Illinois, and his demonstrable qualifications for president were, at best, dubious. His four terms in the Illinois General Assembly, single term in Congress, and position as senior partner in a two-man law firm were all that he could show as proof of leadership or administrative skills. Diarist George Templeton Strong had recorded his concerns regarding Lincoln's qualifications: "The [New-York] Tribune and other papers commend him to popular favor as having had but six months' schooling in his whole life; and because he cut a great many rails, and worked on a flatboat in early youth; all which is somehow presumptive evidence of his statesmanship."

Strong and many others would have preferred to see someone with proven leadership experience, such as former governor of New York William H. Seward,[5] at the helm during these stormy times. But the American people had chosen Lincoln, the one who had spoken so eloquently about the nation's need to "re-adopt the Declaration of Independence" and halt the spread of slavery into the western territories. Lincoln, whose campaign image was the "Rail Splitter," had become the man who answered the North's call for a tough, fair-minded leader.

The people would soon learn that Lincoln had the same basic characteristics as president that he had while he was a simple citizen of the prairies. He still loved the people, had a strong sense of justice, and wanted to help the less fortunate. Added to these qualities was his firm conviction that he had a "most solemn" oath that was "registered in heaven" to preserve the integrity of the United States of America.

Before Lincoln was sworn in, the South's political leaders had pursued their plans for independence by adopting a provisional constitution, appointing Jefferson Davis their president, and declaring themselves a new nation called the Confederate States of America. The Confederate authorities confiscated federal property in the South, including forts, arsenals, and naval facilities. By the time Lincoln took office,

---

5   Seward had held several political offices, including governor of New York. He had been the Republican front-runner for the president, but Lincoln won the nomination in Chicago.

he realized the North would have to make a stand some-where, and he decided to draw the line at Fort Sumter in Charleston, South Carolina. Sumter was located on an island in the middle of Charleston harbor, and its isolation from the mainland offered some hope of successful resistance to military assault.

Southern forces attacked Fort Sumter on April 12, and its small garrison surrendered after thirty hours of bombard-ment. Lincoln called for the states to provide troops to put down the rebellion, which resulted in four more southern states joining the Confederacy.

The dreaded war had begun. Americans wondered whether this untried president had the mettle to lead the North to victory, and they came in droves to the White House to see him for themselves. They wanted to talk to him, offer advice, volunteer to serve—and, for some, seek favors and patronage jobs.

When people first met President Lincoln, they almost always had the same initial impressions of him. First, they were stunned—and a little intimidated—by his physical stature. Second, they were disappointed by the melan-choly demeanor and homely appearance he first presented. But then, when he spoke, they were pleasantly surprised. One acquaintance said, "whenever he began to talk his eyes flashed and every facial movement helped express his idea and feeling. Then involuntarily vanished [on the part of the listener] all thought or consciousness of his uncouth appearance, or his awkward manner, or even his high keyed, unpleasant voice. It required a critical effort of the will to divert attention to the man himself or anything about him, away from the substance of what he was saying."

If the situation called for it, Lincoln would quickly reach out his hand and give the visitor one of his "legendary" handshakes. With these, he would hold his guest's hand for a moment, look them in the eye, and make them feel, as the former slave and famous abolitionist Frederick Douglass would say, that they "were in the presence of a big brother, and that there was safety in his atmosphere." Another who met Lincoln, Robert Brewster Stanton, said, "That first warm hand-clasp from that good and great man is one of the most cherished memories of my life."

If the visitor was a woman or young lady, Lincoln was the perfect model of courtesy, asking them to take a seat when they arrived and then "bowing them out" when they departed. Young girls he frequently called "Sis," and young boys were usually "my son" or "my boy." He knew how to quickly put children at ease. It was not unheard of to see the president of the United States sharing a laugh with some toddler who he was tossing up into the air.

English journalist Edward Dicey wrote that "it was

strange to me to witness the terms of perfect equality on which [President Lincoln] appeared to be with everybody. Occasionally some of his interlocutors called him 'Mr. President,' but the habit was to address him simply as 'Sir.' There was nothing in his own manner, or in that of his guests, to have shown a stranger that the President of the United States was one of the company."

A friend of Lincoln's said "he very much disliked to be called 'Mr. President.' He didn't even like to be called 'Mr.'" When in the company of old friends, "he preferred plain 'Lincoln.'"

Yet in spite of all his nonchalance and friendly manner, Lincoln maintained an air of dignity and respect. Journalist Charles A. Dana said, "Even in his freest moments one always felt the presence of a will and an intellectual power which maintained the ascendancy of the President. He never posed or put on airs or attempted to make any particular impression; but he was always conscious of his own ideas and purposes, even in his most unreserved moments." Journalist Don Piatt, who had known Lincoln since his Springfield days and was not always on the best terms with the president, nevertheless admitted "there was something about Abraham Lincoln that enforced respect. No man presumed on the apparent invitation to be other than respectful."[6] One of Lincoln's secretaries, John

6   For further information on Piatt's relationship with Lincoln, see William C. Harris, *Lincoln and the Border States*, 172.

Hay, observed that "the evidence of all the men admitted to his intimacy is that he maintained, without the least effort of assumption, a singular dignity and reserve in the midst of his easiest conversation."

As the following stories illustrate, people who saw President Lincoln found the experience to be one of the most memorable events of their lives. Their descriptions of him are often a curious blend of compliment and contrast—he was ungainly, yet dignified; awkward, yet graceful; humble, yet grand.

Fifteen-year-old Robert Brewster Stanton first heard Abraham Lincoln speak when the president delivered his first inaugural address on March 4, 1861. He had previously read that Lincoln was an uncouth, awkward man, and he expected to be disappointed when Lincoln walked up to the podium to deliver his speech. Brewster, young man that he was, knew that the hopes of the nation, as well as an entire race, rested upon the leadership of the man who appeared on the Capitol podium before him. As the following account demonstrates, Brewster became personally acquainted with President Lincoln later in the war and had many opportunities to observe him.

There I saw a tall, square-shouldered man with long

arms and legs, but, as he came down the east steps of the Capitol and onto the platform from which he spoke, he walked with such a dignified carriage and seeming perfect ease, that there was dispelled forever from my mind the idea that he was in any way uncouth or at a loss to know the proper thing to do or how to do it.

When he began to speak I was again surprised, on account of what I heard of him. He spoke so naturally, without any attempted oratorical effect, but with such an earnest simplicity and firmness, that he seemed to me to have but one desire as shown in his manner of speaking—to draw that crowd close to him and talk to them as man to man.

His manner was that of perfect self-possession. He seemed to me to fully appreciate his new and unexpected surroundings, to understand perfectly the enormous responsibilities he was undertaking, but at the same time to have perfect confidence in himself that, with God's help, which he always invoked, he could and would carry them through to a successful conclusion...

It was, however, when sitting close to him in his office, listening to those animated and earnest discussions, as well as on other occasions, that I learned to know him and understand, as I thought, his almost every movement.

When sitting in his chair in quiet repose, leaning back listening to others; when he was preparing to reply, as he straightened up and even leaned forward; or while pacing the floor listening or speaking, I never saw him once when, as was so often said, he seemed in the least at a loss to know what to do with his hands or how to carry his large feet. His every movement, his every gesture, seemed so natural, so simple, so unconscious, and yet so suited to the matter in hand and the circumstances at the time, that they impressed me as singularly graceful. Graceful may seem to some a rather strong word to use.

It is true that his figure was tall, lean, possibly lank, and in a sense "ungainly." Yet with all this he had that dignity of bearing, that purposeful, self-possessed, and natural pose which, to me, not only demanded admiration but inspired reverence on almost every occasion. In intimate association, the movements of his body and the gestures of his arms and hands were so pleasing that all impressions of ungainliness were swept away. So I say, Mr. Lincoln was singularly graceful...

Mr. Lincoln's walk, whether while quietly

moving about his office, on the street, or on more stately occasions, was most dignified, easy, natural, and pleasing. His head was usually bent a trifle forward yet not bowed, except on special occasions. There was, to me at least, no evidence of loose joints, jerky movement, or clumsiness. At one time I saw him under circumstances which, if any could bring out those reputed defects in his carriage, should have done so. It was at a meeting of the Houses of Congress, gathered in the House of Representatives to celebrate some victory of the war. The chamber was packed, and the galleries overflowed with men and women. I sat in a front-row seat. The door opened on the opposite side, and as the Marine Band played "Hail to the Chief," Mr. Lincoln entered. The whole audience rose and cheered. He glanced up at the throng and there appeared on his countenance a bright, beautiful, but gentle smile of thanks, nothing more. In a moment this was gone, and holding himself perfectly erect, with an expression of unconcern and self-possession, he walked across the hall up to the speaker's desk with a simple grandeur and profound, dignity that would be difficult for anyone to surpass...

If the matter in hand was of a lighter vein, the same awakening came, but the brighter light of his face turned into that charming smile, gentle, evasive, or sparkling and humorous, which always appeared to me so bewitching. So, whenever I happened to be near him and at first saw that sorrowful, depressed, faraway expression we have heard so much about and which under the burdens he was bearing did darken his face frequently, I had only to wait, sometimes only moments, until the real spirit of the man, his hopefulness, his trustfulness, his cheerfulness, returned and each feature regained its share of that real beauty of soul that shone through them, which held me and everyone who knew him so firmly and drew me to him by some very natural yet magical power that swept away every impression and memory of his appearance except that of beauty.

Jane Grey Swisshelm was a journalist, publisher, abolitionist, advocate for women's rights, and volunteer nurse at army hospitals. Early in the war, she was dissatisfied with Lincoln because he had not freed the slaves. But he issued the

Emancipation Proclamation on January 1, 1863, and so she somewhat reluctantly went to the White House to meet him in February of that year. She later recorded that although she still had "a feeling of scorn" for Lincoln, when she saw him, this changed immediately.

[I was] startled to find a chill of awe pass over me as my eyes rested upon him. It was as if I had suddenly passed a turn in a road and come into full view of the Matterhorn; as if I had stepped from a close room into a mountain breeze.

I have always been sensitive to the atmosphere of those I met, but have never found that of any one impress me as did that of Mr. Lincoln, and I know no word save "grandeur" which expresses the quality of that atmosphere. I think that to me no familiarity, no circumstance, could have made him other than grand. The jests, the sallies, with which he amused small people and covered his own greatness, were the shrubs on the mountain side, the flowers which shot up in the crevices of the rocks! They were no part of the mountain. Grandly and alone he walked his way through this life; and the world had no honors, no emoluments, no reproaches, no shames, no punishments which he could not have borne without swerving or bias.

———◆———

NOAH BROOKS, A JOURNALIST who had known President Lincoln since the Springfield days, became very close to Lincoln and Mary during the war and, according to one historian, was like a surrogate son.[7] In the last two and a half years of the war, he saw the president "almost daily," and he here describes his observations of Lincoln as president when visitors first saw him in the White House.

Breakfast over, by nine o'clock he has directed that the gate which lets in the people shall be opened upon him, and then the multitude of cards, notes and messages which are in the hands of his usher come in upon him. Of course, there can be no precedence, except so far as the President makes it; and, as a majority of the names sent in are new to him, it is very much of a lottery as to who shall get in first. The name being given to the usher by the President, that functionary shows in the gratified applicant, who may have been cooling his heels outside for five minutes or five days, but is now ushered into a large square room, furnished with green stuff, hung around with maps and plans, with a bad portrait of [President Andrew]

7   Burlingame, *Lincoln Observed*, 1.

Jackson over the chimney piece, a writing table piled up with documents and papers, and two large, draperied windows looking out upon the broad Potomac, and commanding the Virginia heights opposite, on which numberless military camps are whitening in the sun.

The President sits at his table and kindly greets whoever comes... With admirable patience and kindness, Lincoln hears his applicant's requests, and at once says what he will do, though he usually asks several questions, generally losing more time than most business men will by trying to understand completely each case, however unimportant, which comes before him. He is not good at dispatching business, but lets every person use more time than he might if the interview were strictly limited to the real necessities of the case. Consequently Lincoln cannot see a tithe of the people who daily besiege his ante-chamber; and, in his anxiety to do equal and exact justice to all, he excludes or delays those who might see him sooner if he did not try to do so much. No man living has a kinder heart than Abraham Lincoln, and all who meet him go away thoroughly impressed with the preponderance of those two lovable and noble traits of his character.

———— ◆◆◆ ————

JOURNALIST AND POET WALT Whitman saw or "passed a word" with the president "twenty or thirty times" during the war, usually when Lincoln was passing by on horseback or traveling in a barouche. Although they did not talk very much, Whitman observed Lincoln with the artist's eye, and the president would later be the subject of some of Whitman's most widely acclaimed poetry, such as "Oh Captain! My Captain!" and "When Lilacs Last in the Dooryard Bloomed." Whitman recorded the following impressions of the president.

I see the President almost every day, as I happen to live where he passes to or from his lodgings out of town. He never sleeps at the White House during the hot season, but has quarters at a healthy location, some three miles north of the city, the Soldiers' Home, a United States military establishment. I saw him this morning about 8:30 coming in to business, riding on Vermont Avenue, near L Street. He always has a company of twenty-five or thirty cavalry, with sabres drawn, and held upright over their shoulders. The party makes no great show in uniforms or horses. Mr. Lincoln, on the saddle, generally rides a good-sized, easy-going gray horse, is dress'd in plain black, somewhat rusty and dusty; wears a black stiff hat, and looks about as ordinary in attire, &c., as the commonest man... I see very plainly Abraham Lincoln's dark brown face, with the deep cut lines, the eyes, &c., always to me with a latent sadness in the expression.

...None of the artists or pictures have caught the subtle and indirect expression of this man's face. One of the great portrait painters of two or three centuries ago is needed.

Abraham Lincoln's was really one of those characters, the best of which is the result of long trains of cause and effect—needing a certain spaciousness of time, and perhaps even remoteness, to properly enclose them—having unequaled influence on the shaping of this Republic (and therefore the world) as to-day, and then far more important in the future. Thus the time has by no means yet come for a thorough measurement of him. Nevertheless, we who live in his era—who have seen him, and heard him, face to face, and are in the midst of, or just parting from, the strong and strange events which he and we have had to do with, can in some respects bear valuable, perhaps indispensable testimony concerning him...

Considered from contemporary points of

view—who knows what the future may decide?—and from the points of view of current Democracy and The Union (the only thing like passion or infatuation in the man was the passion for the Union of These States), Abraham Lincoln seems to me the grandest figure yet, on all the crowded canvas of the Nineteenth Century.

—————

In March 1862, the novelist Nathaniel Hawthorne visited Washington and Union-held regions of Virginia such as Alexandria and Harper's Ferry. He had the good fortune to accompany a deputation that visited the White House to see the president. Hawthorne wrote an article for the Atlantic *magazine of these experiences and included the following description of his visit with Lincoln, part of which an overzealous editor deleted prior to publication, thinking it not "tasteful" to print. Some of the deleted portions are included here, within brackets.*

By and by there was a little stir on the staircase and in the passageway, and in lounged a tall, loose-jointed figure, of an exaggerated Yankee port and demeanor, whom (as being about the homeliest man I ever saw, yet by no means repulsive or disagreeable) it was impossible not to recognize as Uncle Abe... There is no describing his lengthy awkwardness, nor the uncouthness of his movement; and yet it seemed as if I had been in the habit of seeing him daily, and had shaken hands with him a thousand times in some village street; so true was he to the aspect of the pattern American, though with a certain extravagance which, possibly, I exaggerated still further by the delighted eagerness with which I took it in. If put to guess his calling and livelihood, I should have taken him for a country schoolmaster as soon as anything else. He was dressed in a rusty black frock-coat and pantaloons, unbrushed, and worn so faithfully that the suit had adapted itself to the curves and angularities of his figure, and had grown to be an outer skin of the man. He had shabby slippers on his feet. His hair was black, still unmixed with gray, stiff, somewhat bushy, and had apparently been acquainted with neither brush nor comb that morning after the disarrangement of the pillow; and as to a nightcap Uncle Abe probably knows nothing of such effeminacies. His complexion is dark and sallow, betokening, I fear, an insalubrious atmosphere around the White House; he has thick black eyebrows and an impending brow; his nose is large, and the lines about his mouth are very strongly defined.

[The whole physiognomy is as coarse a one as you would meet anywhere in the length and breadth of the States; but, withal, it is redeemed, illuminated, softened, and brightened by a kindly though serious look out of his eyes, and an expression of homely sagacity, that seems weighted with rich results of village experience. A great deal of native sense; no bookish cultivation, no refinement; honest at heart, and thoroughly so, and yet, in some sort, sly—at least, endowed with a sort of tact and wisdom that are akin to craft, and would impel him, I think, to take an antagonist in flank, rather than to make a bull-run at him right in front. But, on the whole, I liked this sallow, queer, sagacious visage, with the homely human sympathies that warmed it; and, for my small share in the matter, would as lief have Uncle Abe for a ruler as any man whom it would have been practicable to put in his place.]

———◆———

BRITISH JOURNALIST WILLIAM HOWARD Russell is known today as one of the first true war correspondents, having covered the Crimean War and then the American Civil War from both the northern and southern viewpoints. Russell's following description of his first sight of President Lincoln balances an amusing description of the outer man with a sincere respect for the inner.

Soon afterwards there entered, with a shambling, loose, irregular, almost unsteady gait, a tall, lank, lean man, considerably over six feet in height, with stooping shoulders, long pendulous arms, terminating in hands of extraordinary dimensions, which, however, were far exceeded in proportion by his feet. He was dressed in an ill-fitting, wrinkled suit of black, which put one in mind of an undertaker's uniform at a funeral; round his neck a rope of black silk was knotted in a large bulb, with flying ends projecting beyond the collar of his coat; his turned-down shirt-collar disclosed a sinewy muscular yellow neck, and above that, nestling in a great black mass of hair, bristling and compact like a ruff of mourning pins, rose the strange quaint face and head, covered with its thatch of wild republican hair, of President Lincoln. The impression produced by the size of his extremities, and by his flapping and wide projecting ears, may be removed by the appearance of kindliness, sagacity, and the awkward bonhommie of his face; the mouth is absolutely prodigious; the lips, straggling and extending almost from one line of black beard to the other, are only kept in order by two deep furrows from the nostril to the chin; the nose itself—a prominent organ—stands out from the face, with an inquiring, anxious air, as though it were sniffing for some good thing in the wind; the eyes dark, full, and deeply set, are penetrating, but full of an expression which almost amounts to tenderness; and above them projects the shaggy brow, running into the small hard frontal space, the development of which can scarcely be estimated accurately, owing to the irregular flocks of thick hair carelessly brushed across it. One would say that, although the mouth was made to enjoy a joke, it could also utter the severest sentence which the head could dictate, but that Mr. Lincoln would be ever more willing to temper justice with mercy, and to enjoy what he considers the amenities of life, than to take a harsh view of men's nature and of the world, and to esti-mate things in an ascetic or puritan spirit.

PEOPLE HEARD OF LINCOLN'S generosity and were not hesitant to stop him on the street in order to ask a favor or voice a complaint. Private soldiers might ask him for their back pay. An office seeker might pester him for an appointment. A soldiers' wife might ask him to have her wounded husband transferred to a different hospital. Lincoln usually listened patiently, then took out his pencil and wrote a note on a card or piece of paper, referring the request to the appropriate government agency and guaranteeing action with his personal signature.

Lincoln was hardly ever accompanied by more than one attendant when he walked to government buildings near the White House, and unless he was traveling across town, he rarely had a military guard with him. So it was no surprise to Lincoln's associate, Francis Bicknell Carpenter, when he saw the president near the White House, unattended, talking to a passerby.

Presently I caught sight of his unmistakable figure standing half-way between the portico and the gateway leading to the War Department, leaning against the iron fence—one arm thrown over the railing, and one foot on the stone coping which supports it, evidently having been intercepted, on his way in from the War Department, by a plain-looking man, who was giving him, very diffidently, an account of a difficulty which he had been unable to have rectified. While waiting, I walked out leisurely to the President's side. He said very little to the man, but was intently studying the expression of his face while he was narrating his trouble. When he had finished, Mr. Lincoln said to him, "Have you a blank card?" The man searched his pockets, but finding none, a gentleman standing near, who had overheard the question, came forward and said,

"Here is one, Mr. President." Several persons had in the meantime gathered around. Taking the card and a pencil, Mr. Lincoln sat down upon the low stone coping, presenting almost the appearance of sitting upon the pavement itself, and wrote an order upon the card to the proper official to "examine this man's case." While writing this, I observed several persons passing down the promenade smiling, at what I presume they thought the undignified appearance of the head of the nation, who, however, seemed utterly unconscious, either of any impropriety in the action, or of attracting any attention. To me it was not only another picture of the native goodness of the man, but of true nobility of character, exemplified not so much by a disregard of conventionalities, as in unconsciousness that there could be any breach of etiquette or dignity in the manner of an honest attempt to serve or secure justice to a citizen of the Republic, however humble he might be.

MOST AMERICANS REALIZED THAT their president was under tremendous pressure and that the day-to-day trials he faced during the war were overwhelming. They could see for themselves how *much he aged over the course of the war, and if they had been able to observe the following scene of Lincoln in the White House, awaiting the results of a terrible battle in 1864, they would have understood the reasons why. It is described by eyewitness Francis Bicknell Carpenter.*

During the first week of the battles of the Wilderness he scarcely slept at all. Passing through the main hall of the domestic apartment on one of these days, I met him, clad in a long morning wrapper, pacing back and forth a narrow passage leading to one of the windows, his hands behind him, great black rings under his eyes, his head bent forward on his breast—altogether such a picture of the effects of sorrow, care, and anxiety as would have melted the hearts of the worst of his adversaries, who so mistakenly applied to him the epithets of tyrant and usurper.

<hr />

Sergeant Smith Stimmel was a part of the army security detail that guarded the White House during the war, and he was frequently with the president. He had developed a sincere respect for Lincoln before the war, having heard him speak when he was still a candidate for office. In listening to what Lincoln said,

Stimmel, like so many others, became convinced "that his mission was to serve all the people of the whole nation, and not a part only." Here he makes note of one touching scene he observed of the most powerful man in the country, talking with some little children outside the White House.

Never did I see Lincoln so full of grief or of his own affairs that he was not ready to sympathize with all who needed him, especially if a child called for help. I think he never passed by a child without a smile, and some way, in spite of sad eyes and heavy brows, the children always took to him. One morning, when the President came over from the War Department, some little school children were playing on the front steps of the White House. He stopped and had a word of pleasantry with them, took one or two of their books and glanced through them, and while he did so, the children crowded around him as if he had been their father.

CHAPTER THREE
KINDNESS PERSONIFIED

———◆◆◆———

AFTER LINCOLN TOOK OFFICE, the White House was besieged by an army of visitors and office seekers intent on speaking with the president. They waited in the stairwells, the hallways, and the anteroom outside of Lincoln's office on the second floor. Lincoln referred to the resulting interviews as his "public opinion baths," welcomed all meetings with visitors, and initially rejected efforts by his staff to put limits on the visiting hours. He said, "I feel—though the tax on my time is heavy—that no hours of my day are better employed than those which thus bring me again within the direct contact and atmosphere of the average of our whole people."

But as the months wore on and the number of visitors didn't diminish, Lincoln finally relented and allowed his private secretaries to establish limited visiting hours. At first, they cut them back to two days a week from 10:00 a.m. to 3:00 p.m., and as Lincoln's wartime responsibilities grew more onerous, they shortened them again to three hours for each session. But the sympathetic Lincoln was never satisfied with these limitations and told one of his private secretaries "they don't want much, and don't get but little, and I *must* see them." He continued to break the rules almost as quickly as his secretaries made them.

The most prolific and persistent of Lincoln's visitors in the early months of the war were the office seekers. The civil service system, which would one day employ those necessary for the daily operation of government, had not been established yet. Consequently, each new presidential administration was responsible for filling these "patronage" job positions. Lincoln was the first president the Republican Party put in office, and party leaders expected him to replace the holdover Democratic bureaucrats with the Republican Party faithful.

As the months passed, these patronage jobs were filled and the number of office seekers shrank, but the number of visitors remained constant. These visitors—soldiers, the mothers or wives of soldiers, war widows, and the elderly— were usually there to seek help because of the hardships of war. One of the assistant secretaries to the president, Edward Duffield Neill, observed that "no one was too poor to be received."

Three decades after the Civil War, former Union general Carl Schurz wrote an essay about Lincoln's character.

He said Lincoln's charm "flowed from the rare depth and genuineness of his convictions and his sympathetic feelings. Sympathy was the strongest element in his nature." According to Schurz, "As his sympathy went forth to others, it attracted others to him. Especially those whom he called the 'plain people' felt themselves drawn to him by the instinctive feeling that he understood, esteemed, and appreciated them. He had grown up among the poor, the lowly, the ignorant. He never ceased to remember the good souls he had met among them, and the many kindnesses they had done him. Although in his mental development he had risen far above them, he never looked down upon them. How they felt and how they reasoned he knew, for so he had once felt and reasoned himself."

It is true that even as president, Lincoln still loved to do favors for people. But now, instead of delivering dry goods to a farmer's wife or chopping wood for an old widow as he did in New Salem, he was saving men's lives and providing life-sustaining aid to the helpless. He told his close friend Joshua Speed that making visitors happy was sometimes the most gratifying aspect of his job.

Lincoln's kindness and sympathetic nature became one of the hallmarks of his presidency, as is evidenced by the following accounts of people who became forever indebted to him.

FRANCIS BICKNELL CARPENTER, AN artist, spent six months in the White House in 1864, studying Lincoln and his cabinet members for the purpose of painting a huge portrait of the president's first reading of the Emancipation Proclamation to his cabinet. While in the White House, Carpenter became an avid observer of Lincoln's daily life in the executive mansion. Carpenter said, "There was a satisfaction to me, differing from that of any other experience, in simply sitting with him. Absorbed in his papers, he would become unconscious of my presence, while I intently studied every line and shade of expression in that furrowed face. In repose, it was the saddest face I ever knew. There were days when I could scarcely look into it without crying."

Carpenter was overwhelmed by Lincoln's kindness and later published a book about this experience, full of anecdotes of the president's meetings with people who needed his help. One of these stories is about a Mr. "M" who had been present during Lincoln's conversation with a woman who had come to ask for a great favor.

"I was waiting my turn to speak to the President one day..." said Mr. M——, "when my attention was attracted by the sad patient face of a woman advanced in life, who in a faded hood and shawl was among the applicants for an interview.

"Presently Mr. Lincoln turned to her, saying in his accustomed manner, 'Well, my good woman, what can I do for you this morning?' 'Mr. President,' said she, 'my husband and three sons all went into the army. My husband was killed in the fight at ———. I get along very badly since then, living all alone, and I thought I would come and ask you to release to me my oldest son.' Mr. Lincoln looked into her face a moment, and in his kindest accents responded, 'Certainly! Certainly! If you have given us *all*, and your prop has been taken away, you are justly entitled to one of your boys!' He immediately made out an order discharging the young man, which the woman took, and thanking him gratefully, went away.

"I had forgotten the circumstance," continued M———, "till last week, when happening to be here again, who should come in but the same woman. It appeared that she had gone herself to the front, with the President's order, and found the son she was in search of had been mortally wounded in a recent engagement, and taken to a hospital. She found the hospital, but the boy was dead, or died while she was there. The surgeon in charge made a memorandum of the facts upon the back of the President's order; and almost broken-hearted, the poor woman had found her way again into Mr. Lincoln's presence.

"He was much affected by her appearance and story, and said: 'I know what you wish me to do now, and I shall do it without your asking; I shall release to you your second son.' Upon this, he took up his pen and commenced writing the order. While he was writing, the poor woman stood by his side, the tears running down her face, and passed her hand softly over his head, stroking his rough hair, as I have seen a fond mother caress a son. By the time he had finished writing, his own heart and eyes were full. He handed her the paper: 'Now,' said he, 'you have one and I one of the other two left: that is no more than right.' She took the paper, and reverently placing her hand again upon his head, the tears still upon her cheeks, said 'The Lord bless you, Mr. Lincoln. May you live a thousand years, and may you always be the head of this great nation!'"

AT THE WAR'S INCEPTION, Lincoln's goal was the preservation of the Union rather than the immediate abolishment of slavery.

But in the second year of the war, Lincoln announced the preliminary Emancipation Proclamation, which would free all slaves in the rebellious southern states, effective January 1, 1863. Black men, including former slaves, started enlisting in the Union army to help fight for their people's freedom.

The famous abolitionist and former slave Frederick Douglass was one of the first African Americans to visit Lincoln in the White House. Although Douglass, like virtually all African Americans at the time, had been elated with Lincoln's Emancipation Proclamation, he nevertheless was not completely satisfied with the government's policies toward black soldiers and had become concerned that they were not being treated equally with whites. In August of 1863, Douglass had his first visit with Lincoln at the White House, and in this meeting, he wanted assurances from the president on several important issues before he would commit to further efforts to recruit black troops. Douglass would soon discover that Lincoln was slowly progressing from being simply a kind man who wanted to end slavery to one who had a growing interest in equal rights for African Americans.

I shall never forget my first interview with this great man. I was accompanied to the executive mansion and introduced to President Lincoln by Senator Pomeroy. The room in which he received visitors was the one now used by the president's secretaries. I entered it with a moderate estimate of my own consequence, and yet there I was to talk with, and even to advise, the head man of a great nation. Happily for me, there was no vain pomp and ceremony about him. I was never more quickly or more completely put at ease in the presence of a great man, than in that of Abraham Lincoln. He was seated, when I entered, in a low arm chair, with his feet extended on the floor, surrounded by a large number of documents, and several busy secretaries. The room bore the marks of business, and the persons in it, the President included, appeared to be much over-worked and tired. Long lines of care were already deeply written on Mr. Lincoln's brow, and his strong face, full of earnestness, lighted up as soon as my name was mentioned. As I approached and was introduced to him, he rose and extended his hand, and bade me welcome. I at once felt myself in the presence of an honest man—one whom I could love, honor, and trust without reserve or doubt. Proceeding to tell him who I was, and what I was doing, he promptly, but kindly, stopped me, saying: "I know who you are, Mr. Douglass; Mr. Seward has told me all about you. Sit down. I am glad to see you." I then told him the object of my visit: that I was assisting to raise colored troops; that several months before I had been very successful in getting men to enlist, but that now it was not easy to induce the colored men to enter the service, because there was a feeling among them that the government did not deal fairly with them in several respects. Mr. Lincoln asked me to state particulars...

Mr. Lincoln listened with patience and silence to all I had to say. He was serious and even troubled by what I had said, and by what he had evidently thought himself before upon the same points. He impressed me with the solid gravity of his character, by his silent listening, not less than by his earnest reply to my words...

Though I was not entirely satisfied with his views, I was so well satisfied with the man and with the educating tendency of the conflict, I determined to go on with the recruiting.

True to his word, Lincoln later addressed all of Douglass's concerns, which primarily dealt with equal pay and treatment for black soldiers, when it became politically feasible to do so.

Douglass met Lincoln two more times before the war ended and would later say that Abraham Lincoln was the only man who "in no single instance reminded me of the difference between himself and myself, of the difference of color." He would also say that "I felt in his presence I was in the presence of a very great man, as great as the greatest, I felt as though I could go and put my hand on him if I wanted to, to put my hand on his shoulder."

IN THE CIVIL WAR, it was a common occurrence for brothers, cousins, fathers, and sons to join the same regiment and share its trials for the duration of the war. Although soldiers were supposed to be at least eighteen years old, younger boys frequently lied about their age, obtained permission from their parents to join, or ran away to join other units under assumed names. Regimental drummers were considered "musicians," not combatants, so boys as young as ten or twelve marched alongside soldiers. Although these drummer boys did not carry rifles, they were, tragically, sometimes among the battle casualties.

The following is an account of a young regimental drummer who, having heard of Lincoln's kindness, came to the White House, believing the president was his last hope. The story was told by Francis Bicknell Carpenter.

Among a large number of persons waiting in the room to speak with Mr. Lincoln, on a certain day in November, '64, was a small, pale, delicate-looking boy about thirteen years old. The President saw him standing, looking feeble and faint, and said: "Come here, my boy, and tell me what you want." The boy advanced, placed his hand on the arm of the President's chair, and with bowed head and timid accents said: "Mr. President, I have been a drummer in a regiment for two years, and my colonel got angry with me and turned me off. I was taken sick, and have been a long time in hospital. This is the first time I have been out, and I came to see if you could not do something for me." The President looked at him kindly and tenderly, and asked him where he lived. "I have no home," answered the boy. "Where is your father?" "He died in the army," was the reply. "Where is your mother?" continued the President. "My mother is dead also. I have no mother, no father, no brothers, no sisters, and," bursting into tears, "no friends—nobody cares for me." Mr. Lincoln's eyes filled with tears, and he said to him, "Can't you sell newspapers?" "No," said the boy, "I am too weak; and the surgeon of the hospital told me I must leave, and I have no money, and no place to go to." The scene was wonderfully affecting. The President drew forth a card, and addressing on it certain officials to whom his request was law, gave

special directions "to care for this poor boy." The wan face of the little drummer lit up with a happy smile as he received the paper, and he went away convinced that he had one good and true friend, at least, in the person of the President.

IN ADDITION TO PERSONAL meetings with visitors in his office at the White House, Lincoln spent countless hours greeting people in reception lines during formal receptions in the White House's East

Room. Although each encounter was very short—little more than a greeting and handshake—Lincoln was able to talk to a much larger number of people this way. The crowd represented quite a menagerie from Washington society, but it didn't matter to the president who they were. With a kind smile, he politely greeted everyone, and one of Lincoln's private secretaries, William O. Stoddard, recorded this brief glimpse of the president in the reception line.

In no other land, or place, or time could there be gathered such a miscellaneous assortment of life and character as is now passing before Father Abraham.

A volunteer in the uniform of a private soldier is at this moment towering in front of him, and the hand of welcome which at once goes out is met by a weaker grasp than is expected. The man's face was pale, but it flushes.

"You're just a peg taller'n I am, Mr. Lincoln, but I reckon I'd ha' outweighed you 'fore I went into hospital."

"Where were you wounded?" asks the President, with evident interest.

"Reckon it was all over me. 'Twas one of these 'ere Potomac fevers."

"Worse than a bullet," responds Mr. Lincoln; "but it must have taken a heap of fever to go all over you."

"Well, it did!" The soldier swings cheerily on, with something to tell in camp, and he has hardly hindered the procession.

"I voted for you, Mr. Lincoln," chirps a short, fat, honest-faced man, who pauses in front of him. "I—I'm glad I did. I—I'd do it again. I—I'm putting in an application for paymaster. I—"

"Want to be a paymaster, eh?" laughs the President. "Well, some people would rather take money in than pay it out. It would about kill some men I know to make paymasters of 'em."

If that man meant to say any more he has lost his chance, for the President bends suddenly, and his long arm reaches through the press.

"Come here, sister. I can't let you pass me in that way."

Sunny curls, blue eyes, cheeks delicately rosy, a child of seven or eight, warmly but plainly dressed, and now she is trembling with shyness and pleasure as he draws her to him for a kiss and to pat her golden hair. All children are favorites of his, and as she is released his arm goes out again and he has made another capture, but not without a vigorous kicking, and a short, half-frightened squall. Up, up, goes a chubby boy of four, and the squall changes to a boyish laugh, for he is a brave little fellow, and he knows a game of toss, even if it lifts him uncommonly high in the air.

We cannot hear just what the President says, but the children can, and both of them have hurried away, followed by parents and what seems a file of aunts and other relatives, all one chuckle of delight over this rare incident.

That is a noble-looking woman, whose hand the President is taking. Her features are fine, and there is a splendid glow of enthusiasm shining all over her face.

"I have three sons in the army, Mr. Lincoln."

"You may well be proud of that, ma'am."

Her eyes seem growing darker and yet brighter, and her bosom swells more proudly—if it is with pride. She hesitates, a breathing-space, but her lips do not quiver as she adds, quietly, firmly:

"There were four, Mr. Lincoln, but my eldest boy—" and somehow she can say no more and turns to pass onward.

"God bless you, madame," but she does not give him a chance to say any more.

CONGRESSMAN DANIEL W. VOORHEES of Indiana related how, in early 1864, a married couple from Kentucky came to him seeking help. The woman's elderly father had been tricked into carrying medicine to the Confederates, arrested by Union agents, and was scheduled to hang the next day. Voorhees sought the help of one of Indiana's senators, and both of them accompanied the distraught couple on a visit to an obviously fatigued president.

We ascended the stairs and filed into the President's room. As we entered, I saw at a glance that Mr. Lincoln had that sad, preoccupied, far-away look I had so often seen him wear, and during which it was difficult at times to engage his attention to passing events. As we approached he slowly turned to us, inclined his head and spoke. Senator [Henry] Lane at once, in his rapid, nervous style, explained the occasion of our call, and made known our reasons for asking Executive clemency. While he was talking Mr. Lincoln looked at him in a patient, tired sort of way, but not as if he was struck with the sensibilities of the subject as we were. When the

Senator ceased speaking there was no immediate response; on the contrary, rather an awkward pause. My heart beat fast, for in that pause was now my great hope, and I was not disappointed. Mrs. Bullitt had taken a seat on coming in not far from the President, and now, in quivering but distinct tones, she spoke, addressing him as "Mr. Lincoln." He turned to her with a grave, benignant expression, and as he listened his eye lost that distant look, and his face grew animated with a keen and vivid interest. The little pale-faced woman at his side talked wonderfully well for her father's life, and her eyes pleaded even more eloquently than her tongue. Suddenly, and while she was talking, Mr. Lincoln, turning to Senator Lane, exclaimed:

"Lane, what did you say this man's name was?"

"Luckett," answered the Senator.

"Not Henry M. Luckett?" quickly queried the President.

"Yes," interposed Mrs. Bullitt; "my father's name is Henry M. Luckett."

"Why, he preached in Springfield years ago, didn't he?" said Mr. Lincoln, now all animation and interest.

"Yes, my father used to preach in Springfield," replied the daughter.

"Well, this is wonderful!" Mr. Lincoln remarked; and turning to the party in front of him he continued: "I knew this man well; I have heard him preach; he was a tall, angular man like I am, and I have been mistaken for him on the streets. Did you say he was to be shot day after to-morrow? No, no! There will be no shooting nor hanging in this case. Henry M. Luckett! There must be something wrong with him, or he wouldn't be in such a scrape as this. I don't know what more I can do for him, but you can rest assured, my child," turning to Mrs. Bullitt, "that your father's life is safe."

He touched a bell on his table, and the telegraph operator appeared from an adjoining room. To him Mr. Lincoln dictated a dispatch to General Hurlbut, directing him to suspend the execution of Henry M. Luckett and await further orders in the case.

As we thanked him and took our leave, he repeated, as if to himself:

"Henry M. Luckett! No, no! There is no shooting or hanging in this case."

On his way to the War Department's telegraph office early one morning, Lincoln noticed a young woman carrying a baby in her arms, pacing back and forth in the hallway and crying. The president asked Major Eckert, the officer in charge of the telegraph operators, to talk to the woman and determine the cause of her trouble. Eckert complied and reported back to Lincoln that the woman had journeyed to Washington with the belief that she could get a pass to the front lines to see her husband in the Army of the Potomac. She wanted to show him their child, who had been born since the father enlisted, but she found out soldiers' wives were not allowed to visit the army in camp. David Homer Bates, one of the telegraph operators, wrote the following account of Lincoln's attempt to help her.

Lincoln said, "Major, let's send her down." Eckert replied that strict orders had been given not to let women go to the front. [Secretary of War Edwin] Stanton, entering the office at the time and seeing the evident sympathy of Lincoln for the woman in her trouble, said, "Why not give her husband a leave of absence to allow him to see his wife in Washington?" The President replied: "Well, come, let's do that. Major, you write the message."

But Eckert said the order must be given officially, and Lincoln replied: "All right, Major; let Colonel Hardie (Assistant Adjutant-General) write the order and send it by telegraph, so the man can come right up." Colonel Hardie wrote the message, which was telegraphed to the Army of the Potomac, and when the sorrowing woman was informed of what had been done, she came into the office to express her gratitude to the President. Lincoln then asked her where she was stopping. She said that she had not yet found a place, having come direct from the railroad station to the White House, and then to the War Department. Lincoln then directed Eckert to obtain an order from Colonel Hardie to allow the young mother and her baby to be taken care of in Carver Hospital until her husband arrived. This was done, and the soldier was allowed to remain with his wife and child for over a week before returning to his regiment.

LATE IN THE WAR, *the famous former slave Sojourner Truth decided to visit Abraham Lincoln. Truth was a leader in the Underground Railroad and had led many slaves to freedom in the North. She was also a well-known speaker, abolitionist, and advocate of women's rights. Her account of the meeting with President Abraham Lincoln is taken from a letter she dictated to her friend Rowland Johnson.*

It was about 8 o'clock A.M., when I called on the president. Upon entering his reception room we found about a dozen persons in waiting, among them two colored women. I had quite a pleasant time waiting until he was disengaged, and enjoying his conversation with others; he showed as much kindness and consideration to the colored persons as to the whites—if there was any difference, more. One case was that of a colored woman who was sick and likely to be turned out of her house on account of her inability to pay her rent. The president listened with much attention, and spoke to her with kindness and tenderness. He said he had given so much he could give no more, but told her where to go and get the money, and asked Mrs. C—n to assist her, which she did.

The president was seated at his desk. Mrs. C. said to him, "This is Sojourner Truth, who has come all the way from Michigan to see you." He then arose, gave me his hand, made a bow, and said, "I am pleased to see you."

I said to him, Mr. President, when you first took

your seat I feared you would be torn to pieces, for I likened you unto Daniel, who was thrown into the lion's den; and if the lions did not tear you into pieces, I knew that it would be God that had saved you; and I said, if he spared me I would see you before the four years expired, and he has done so, and now I am here to see you for myself.

He then congratulated me upon having been spared. Then I said, I appreciate you, for you are the best president who has ever taken the seat. He replied: "I expect you have reference to my having emancipated the slaves in my proclamation. But," said he, mentioning the names of several of his predecessors (and among them emphatically that of Washington), "they were all just as good, and would have done just as I have done if the time had come. If the people over the river [pointing across the Potomac] had behaved themselves, I could not have done what I have; but they did not, which gave the opportunity to do those things." I then said, I thank God that you were the instrument selected by him and the people to do it. I told him that I had never heard of him before he was talked of for president. He smilingly replied, "I had heard of you many times before that."

He then showed me the Bible presented to him by the colored people of Baltimore, of which you have no doubt seen a description. I have seen it for myself and it is beautiful beyond description. After I had looked it over, I said to him, "This is beautiful indeed; the colored people have given this to the Head of the Government, and that Government once sanctioned laws that would not permit its people to learn enough to enable them to read this Book. And for what? Let them answer who can."

I must say, and I am proud to say, that I never was treated by any one with more kindness and cordiality than were shown to me by that great and good man, Abraham Lincoln, by the grace of God President of the United States for four years more. He took my little book, and with the same hand that signed the death-warrant of slavery, he wrote as follows:

For Aunty Sojourner Truth,

Oct. 29, 1864. A. Lincoln

As I was taking my leave, he arose and took my hand, and said he would be pleased to have me call again. I felt that I was in the presence of a friend, and I now thank God from the bottom of my heart that I always have advocated his cause, and have done it openly and boldly. I shall feel still more in duty bound to do so in time to come. May God assist me.

———◦◦◦———

SOMETIMES, PEOPLE TRAVELED GREAT *distances to see President Lincoln and ask for his help. Mrs. Anna Byers-Jennings traveled from Fairmont, Missouri, to Washington on behalf of a man named Daniel Hayden, who had been captured and confined to a military prison in Alton, Illinois, for over a year. She arrived at the White House after visiting hours and was advised by a man who had just met with the president to go immediately upstairs to see him, since he was currently alone. Mrs. Byers recalled:*

I certainly felt that the old man's advice was good, but it also occurred to me that I would be running a great risk to walk into the private office of President Lincoln, unannounced and uncalled for. I was only a green young woman from the backwoods of Missouri. What would I do if he should order me out, or something of that kind? My case would surely be hopeless and I undone. But the thought of the poor old father who was paying my expenses, and the advice of the clerk whom I met made me somewhat desperate, and after getting up all the courage possible I made my way upstairs and to the door of the office. I could feel my heart beating in an unusual manner, and I was actually trembling from head to foot. At last I took hold of the door knob, hesitated a moment, then turned it and walked in.

Mr. Lincoln was alone, sitting beside a very plain table, resting his elbow on the table, and his head upon his hand...

When I entered he raised his tired eyes, oh so tired, and with a worn look I can never, never forget. As I advanced, and before he spoke, I said: "Mr. Lincoln, you must pardon this intrusion, but I just could not wait any longer to see you." The saintly man then reached out his friendly hand and said: "No intrusion at all, not the least. Sit down, my child, sit down, and let me know what I can do for you." I suggested that probably he was too tired. He replied: "I am tired, but I am waiting to say good-bye to two friends from Chicago, who are going on the train at seven."

I briefly explained to him the case before me, saying that Hayden had been in prison fifteen months; that he was a Union man, forced from his home by the rebels; that his wife had died since he had been in prison, leaving five little children with his very aged mother, who had lately lost her eyesight. I had, besides, a large envelope filled with letters of recommendation from different officers of the Department of Missouri; also a petition drawn up by myself, signed by the Union neighbors of Mr. Hayden; appended to it a certificate of their loyalty, signed by the county clerk, who had affixed the seal of the county court. To all of the above Senator John B. Henderson had been kind enough to add an indorsement for myself, in strong, impressive language.

When I offered my papers to the President he didn't touch them, but said, without raising a hand: "Now, suppose you read them over for me. Your eyes are younger than mine. Besides, as I told you, I am very tired." By accident, the petition was the first thing I took up. When I came to John B. Henderson's name he reached out and said quickly: "Let me see that." As he glanced over it to the bottom, he laid the paper down, slapped his hand upon the table and exclaimed: "Plague on me, if that ain't John Henderson's signature. Well, I'll release this man just because John Henderson asks me to do it. I know he wouldn't ask me if it wasn't right, nor send anyone here that would do anything detrimental to our government. Come in tomorrow at 8 o'clock—mind, at 8 precisely. Bring that petition with John Henderson's name on it and I'll fix it so you can get this man out of prison."

When I told the president I was afraid I wouldn't be admitted to his office in the morning, Lincoln responded, "Oh, the usher is only a slender little

Irishman. If he refuses to let you pass, slap him down the steps, and walk in as you did just now."

THE NEXT MORNING, AFTER being admitted to Lincoln's office, she continued the narrative:

He sat down by his desk, reached out for the petition, wrote across the back, "Release this man on order No. __. A. Lincoln." As he handed it straight back to me he remarked with looks full of inexpressible sympathy and goodness: "Mrs. Byers, that will get your man out. And tell his poor old mother I wish to heaven it was in my power to give her back her eyesight so she might see her son when he gets home to her."

CHAPTER FOUR
"THE BOY SHALL BE PARDONED"

DURING THE CIVIL WAR, soldiers who committed crimes were tried by military courts, known as courts-martial, rather than civilian courts. Each court-martial consisted of a military judge, a prosecutor, a defense counsel, and at least three officers acting as jury. Courts-martial tried soldiers for a myriad of offenses that could range from petty larceny to desertion or murder. Punishment, depending on the crime, might be something as simple as suspension of pay for petty larceny, or death by firing squad for serious crimes such as desertion, sleeping while on guard duty, or cowardice in battle.

Lincoln referred to cowardice in battle as his "leg cases," because "if Almighty God gives a man a cowardly pair of legs how can he help their running away with him?" In examining one such case, he said, "I must put this by until I can settle in my mind whether this soldier can better serve the country dead than living."

Abraham Lincoln attempted to review every court-martial case that had resulted in a soldier being sentenced to death by firing squad or hanging. He would spend hours reading cases one by one, searching for reasons to pardon the men. He sympathized with soldiers who had run away from battle, grew homesick and deserted, or fell asleep on guard duty. He knew that many of them were mere boys, and although the army didn't mind sentencing a boy under eighteen years of age to be shot for dereliction of duty, the president was very reluctant to allow this. He once said that it was very hard to permit a soldier to be shot when he knew that by simply signing his name to a document, the man's life could be spared. One time, admonished by a general for halting the execution of twenty deserters, Lincoln said, "there are already too many weeping widows in the United States. For God's sake, don't ask me to add to the number, for I tell you plainly, I won't do it!"

Lincoln's private secretary John Hay once wrote in his diary, "Today we spent 6 hours deciding on Court martials, the President, Judge Holt & I. I was amused at the eagerness with which the President caught at any fact which would justify him in saving the life of a condemned soldier. He was only merciless in cases where meanness or cruelty were shown."

One time, finding out that a condemned prisoner had been previously wounded in battle, Lincoln quickly asked,

"Did you say this boy was once badly wounded? Then, since the Scriptures say that in the shedding of blood is remission of sins, I guess we'll have to let him off." In another case, he said, "If a man had more than one life I think a little hanging would not hurt this one, but after he is once dead we cannot bring him to life, no matter how sorry we may be; so the boy shall be pardoned."

Knowing Lincoln's sympathetic nature, Attorney General Edward Bates told his pardon clerk, Edmund Stedman, that his [Stedman's] "most important duty was to keep all but the most deserving cases from coming before the kind Mr. Lincoln at all; since there was nothing harder for him to do than to put aside a prisoner's application, and he [the President] could not resist it when it was urged by a pleading wife and a weeping child."

Lincoln was lenient with the boys and men of the army, because he knew that, as volunteer troops, they had not received the months of training and military discipline normally drilled into professional soldiers. He admitted that "some of my generals complain that I impair discipline and subordination in the army by my pardons and respites, but it makes me rested, after a day's hard work if I can find some good excuse for saving a man's life, and I go to bed happy as I think how joyous the signing of my name will make him and his family and friends."

The soldiers who had been condemned to die, being imprisoned, were not able to solicit a pardon from the president themselves. But as the following stories make evident, their pardons were effectively presented to "the kind Mr. Lincoln" by wives, mothers, sisters, and friends.

<hr />

WHEN VISITORS ARRIVED AT the White House, they would advise the attendant of their reasons for coming and then take their place in the waiting room. Although important political leaders and generals were frequently forced to wait, they were almost always able to obtain an audience with the president that same day. For private citizens, since there were so many of them, it was more problematic for those visiting on the grounds of clemency. As the following story demonstrates, if a supplicant for pardon was able to enlist the help of a politician or government official, his or her chances of seeing Lincoln increased. Francis Bicknell Carpenter recorded the following story by former Lieutenant Governor Thomas H. Ford of Ohio, who had an appointment with the president one evening.

As [Ford] entered the vestibule of the White House his attention was attracted by a poorly clad young woman who was violently sobbing. He asked her the cause of her distress. She said that she had been ordered away by the servants, after vainly waiting many hours to see the President about her only brother, who had been condemned to death. Her story was this: She and her brother were foreigners, and orphans. They had been in this country several years. Her brother enlisted in the army, but, through bad influences, was induced to desert. He was captured, tried, and sentenced to be shot—the old story. The poor girl had obtained the signatures of some persons who had formerly known him to a petition for a pardon, and, alone, had come to Washington to lay the case before the President. Thronged as the waiting-rooms always were, she had passed the long hours of two days trying in vain to get an audience, and had at length been ordered away.

Mr. Ford's sympathies were at once enlisted. He said that he had come to see the President, but did not know as *he* should succeed. He told her, however, to follow him up-stairs, and he would see what could be done. Just before reaching the door, Mr. Lincoln came out, and meeting his friend, said good-humoredly, "are you not ahead of time?" Mr. Ford showed his watch, with the pointers upon the hour of six. "Well," replied Mr. Lincoln, "I have been so busy to-day that I have not had time to get a lunch. Go in and sit down; I will be back directly."

Private Edward A. Cary of the 44th
Virginia Regiment and his sister,
Emma J. Garland, née Cary

Mr. Ford made the young woman accompany him into the office, and when they were seated, said to her: "Now, my good girl, I want you to muster all the courage you have in the world. When the President comes back he will sit down in that arm-chair. I shall get up to speak to him, and as I do so you must force yourself between us, and insist upon his examination of your papers, telling him it is a case of life and death, and admits of no delay." These instructions were carried out to the letter. Mr.

Lincoln was at first somewhat surprised at the apparent forwardness of the young woman, but observing her distressed appearance, he ceased conversation with his friend, and commenced an examination of the document she had placed in his hands. Glancing from it to the face of the petitioner, whose tears had broken forth afresh, he studied its expression for a moment, and then his eye fell upon her scanty but neat dress. Instantly his face lighted up. "My poor girl," said he, "you have come here with no governor, or senator, or member of congress, to plead your cause. You seem honest and truthful; and"— with much emphasis—"you don't wear '*hoops*'; and I will be whipped but I will pardon your brother!"

When Lincoln left Springfield for Washington, his friend Ward Hill Lamon volunteered to accompany the president-elect and act as bodyguard. Once in Washington, Lincoln appointed Lamon to the position of marshall for the District of Columbia and frequently gave his trusted friend special assignments. After Lincoln died, Lamon published Recollections of Abraham Lincoln, *which included the following story of Lincoln's willingness to always extend mercy, no matter the hour of the day or night.*

[New York Congressman William A.] Wheeler tells of a young man who had been convicted by a military court of sleeping at his post—a grave offence, for which he had been sentenced to death. He was but nineteen years of age, and the only son of a widowed mother. He had suffered greatly with home-sickness, and overpowered at night with cold and watching, was overcome by sleep. He had always been an honest, faithful, temperate soldier. His comrades telegraphed his mother [to warn her] of his fate. She at once went to [her congressman] Orlando Kellogg, whose kind heart promptly responded to her request, and he left for Washington by the first train. He arrived in that city at midnight. The boy was to be executed on the afternoon of the next day. With the aid of his friend, Mr. Wheeler, he passed the military guard about the White House and reached the door-keeper, who, when he knew Mr. Kellogg's errand, took him to Mr. Lincoln's sleeping-room. Arousing Mr. Lincoln, Mr. Kellogg made known the emergency in a few words. Without stopping to dress, the President went to another room and awakened a messenger. Then sitting down, still in undress, he wrote a telegram to the officer commanding at Yorktown to suspend the execution of the boy until further orders. The telegram was sent at once to the War Department, with directions to the messenger to remain until an answer was received. Getting uneasy at the seeming delay, Mr. Lincoln dressed, went to the Department, and remained until the receipt of his telegram was acknowledged. Then turning to Kellogg, with trembling voice he said, "Now you just telegraph that mother that her boy is safe, and I will go home and go to bed. I guess we shall all sleep better for this night's work."

White House doorkeeper "Old Daniel" told Francis Bicknell Carpenter this story about a poor woman's appeal to Abraham Lincoln for a pardon for her husband. If it weren't for her baby, she might have never seen the president.

A poor woman from Philadelphia had been waiting with a baby in her arms for several days to see the President. It appeared by her story that her husband...in a state of intoxication, was induced to enlist. Upon reaching the post assigned his regiment, he deserted, thinking the government was not entitled to his services. Returning home, he was arrested, tried, convicted, and sentenced to be shot. The sentence was to be executed on a Saturday. On Monday his wife left her home with her baby, to endeavor to see the President. Said Daniel, "She had been waiting here three days, and there was no chance for her to get in. Late in the afternoon of the third day, the President was going through the passage to his private room to get a cup of tea. On the way he heard the baby cry. He instantly went back to his office and rang the bell. "Daniel," said he, "is there a woman with a baby in the anteroom?" I said there was, and if he would allow me to say it, it was a case he ought to see; for it was a matter of life and death. "Send her to me at once." She went in, told her story, and the President pardoned her husband. As the woman came out from his presence, her eyes were lifted and her lips moving in prayer, the tears streaming down her cheeks. Said Daniel, "I went up to her, and pulling her shawl, said, 'Madam, it was the baby that did it.'"

ONE OF THE LAST times Lincoln's close friend Joshua F. Speed saw the president was about ten days before his second inauguration in 1865. Although Speed had remained in Kentucky through *the duration of the war, he had maintained a correspondence with Lincoln, and his older brother James Speed became Lincoln's second attorney general. Long after the war, Speed wrote the following account of Lincoln granting a pardon while he was visiting his old friend in the White House.*

The last interview but one I had with him was about ten days prior to his last inauguration. Congress was drawing to a close; it had been an important session; much attention had to be given to the important bills he was signing; a great war was upon him and the country; visitors were coming and going to the President with their varying complaints and grievances from morning till night with almost as much regularity as the ebb and flow of the tide; and he was worn down in health and spirits. On this occasion I was sent for, to come and see him. Instructions were given that when I came I should be admitted. When I entered his office it was quite full, and many more—among them not a few Senators and members of Congress—still waiting. As soon as I was fairly inside, the President remarked that he desired to see me as soon as he was through giving audiences, and that if I had nothing to do I could take the papers and amuse myself in that or any other way I saw fit till he was ready. In the room, when I entered, I observed sitting near the fireplace, dressed in humble attire, two ladies modestly waiting their turn. One after another of the visitors came and went, each bent on his own particular errand, some satisfied and others evidently displeased at the result of their mission. The hour had arrived to close the door against all further callers. No one was left in the room now except the President, the two ladies, and me. With a rather peevish and fretful air he turned to them and said, "Well, ladies, what can I do for you?" They both commenced to speak at once. From what they said he soon learned that one was the wife and the other the mother of two men imprisoned for resisting the draft in western Pennsylvania. "Stop," said he, "don't say any more. Give me your petition." The old lady responded, "Mr. Lincoln, we've got no petition; we couldn't write one and had no money to pay for writing one, and I thought best to come and see you." "Oh," said he, "I understand your cases." He rang his bell and ordered one of the messengers to tell General Dana to bring him the names of all the men in prison for resisting the draft in western Pennsylvania. The General soon came with the list. He enquired if there was any difference in the charges or degrees of guilt. The General replied that he knew of none. "Well, then," said he, "these fellows have suffered long enough, and I have thought so for some time, and now that my mind is on the subject I believe I will turn out the whole flock. So, draw up the order, General, and I will sign it." It was done and the General left the room. Turning to the women he said, "Now, ladies, you can go." The younger of the two ran forward and was in the act of kneeling in thankfulness. "Get up," he said; "don't kneel to me, but thank God and go." The old lady now came forward with tears in her eyes to express her gratitude. "Good-bye, Mr. Lincoln," said she; "I shall probably never see you again till we meet in heaven." These were her exact words. She had the President's hand in hers, and he was deeply moved. He instantly took her right hand in both of his and, following her to the door, said, "I am afraid with all my troubles I shall never get to the resting-place you speak of; but if I do I am sure I shall find you. That you wish me to get there is, I believe, the best wish you could make for me. Good-bye."

We were now alone. I said to him, "Lincoln,

with my knowledge of your nervous sensibility, it is a wonder that such scenes as this don't kill you." He thought for a moment and then answered in a languid voice, "Yes, you are to a certain degree right. I ought not to undergo what I so often do. I am very unwell now; my feet and hands of late seem to be always cold, and I ought perhaps to be in bed; but things of the sort you have just seen don't hurt me, for, to tell you the truth, that scene is the only thing to-day that has made me forget my condition or given me any pleasure. I have, in that order, made two people happy and alleviated the distress of many a poor soul whom I never expect to see. That old lady," he continued, "was no counterfeit. The mother spoke out in all the features of her face. It is more than one can often say that in doing right one has made two people happy in one day. Speed, die when I may, I want it said of me by those who know me best, that I always plucked a thistle and planted a flower when I thought a flower would grow."

JOHN D. KERNAN, SON *of New York Congressman Francis Kernan, who knew Lincoln during the war, tells this story of a soldier's wife who enlisted the help of Kernan's father to obtain a pardon for her husband. Her husband had been charged with desertion and sentenced to be shot.*

A story my father, the Hon. Francis Kernan, used to tell illustrates Lincoln's kindness of heart. When my father was a member of Congress, during the War, a woman came to him one day and said that her husband had been captured as a deserter and she wanted my father to go and see the President about the matter.

So the next morning he called on Mr. Lincoln. He found him very much occupied, but, sending in word that it was an urgent matter, the President saw him. My father gave the President the facts in the case. It seems that the man had been absent a year from his family and, without leave, had gone home to see them. On his way back to the army he was arrested as a deserter and sentenced to be shot. The sentence was to be carried out that very day. The wife had come on to intercede for her husband.

The President listened attentively, becoming more and more interested in the story. Finally he said: "Why, Kernan, of course this man wanted to see his family; and they oughtn't to shoot him for that." So he immediately rang his bell, called his secretary and gave him orders to send off telegrams suspending the sentence and ordering the record of the case to be sent to him. As he went on dictating to his secretary he became more and more anxious about the matter. He exclaimed: "For God's sake, get that off just as quick as you can, or they will shoot this man in spite of me!" The result was that the man got a pardon and took his place again in the army.

———◆———

ONE OF THE MOST *cantankerous members of Congress during the Civil War was the old chairman of the Ways and Means Committee, Pennsylvania Congressman Thaddeus Stevens. Stevens, known in Congress as "The Dictator," was a radical Republican and a merciless opponent when debating Democrats in the halls of Congress. But even the callous old Stevens had a soft spot, and he once brought to the White House a mother who was seeking a pardon for her son. The story is related by Francis Bicknell Carpenter.*

The Hon. Thaddeus Stevens told me that on one occasion he called at the White House with an elderly lady, in great trouble, whose son had been in the army, but for some offence had been court-martialed, and sentenced either to death, or imprisonment at hard labor for a long term. There were some extenuating circumstances; and after a full hearing, the President turned to the representative, and said: "Mr. Stevens, do you think this is a case which will warrant my interference?" "With my knowledge of the facts and the parties," was the reply, "I should have no hesitation in granting a pardon." "Then," returned Mr. Lincoln, "I will pardon him," and he proceeded forthwith to execute the paper. The gratitude of the mother was too deep for expression, and not a word was said between her and Mr. Stevens until they were half way down the stairs on their passage out, when she suddenly broke forth in an excited manner with the words, "I knew it was a copperhead lie!" "What do you refer to, madam?" asked Mr. Stevens. "Why, they told me he was an ugly looking man," she replied, with vehemence. "He is the handsomest man I ever saw in my life!"

FEW VISITORS WERE MORE fortunate than John M. Bullock, for whom "chance and opportunity" provided a meeting with the president. Bullock wanted to ask that a pardon be granted for his critically ill brother, an unrepentant Confederate soldier who was lying in a Union prison hospital. Normally, Confederate prisoners were not released unless they took the oath of allegiance to the United States. While waiting to see the president, Bullock carefully prepared in his mind a "set speech," which he hoped would convince the president to allow his brother to go home.

Suddenly, the door opened, and the tall form of the President, six feet four inches in height, towered above me. Closing the door quietly behind him, he drew the largest of the easy-chairs to one side of the glowing log fire, and sitting down, leaned his elbow on the arm toward me, and said, "Now, my son, what can I do for you?"... Where now was my set speech? That I never knew. All I saw before me was a kind, sorrowful face, ready to listen to my story. I was not in the least embarrassed, as I supposed I should be, and at once began to tell Mr. Lincoln what I had come to ask of him. I said: "Mr. President, I have come to ask you to parole my brother, Lieutenant Waller R. Bullock, from Johnson's Island, where he is sick and wounded. He is extremely ill, and I want you to release him so that he may be brought home to die." I knew what he would ask me the first thing, and my heart sank as I heard the fateful question put. "Will your brother take the oath [of allegiance to the Union]?" said Mr. Lincoln. "No, sir; he will not," I replied. "He will have to die in prison if that is the only alternative." "I cannot parole him," said the President. "I should like to do so; but it is impossible unless he will take the oath." I replied: "Mr. Lincoln, my brother is very ill, and cannot live long in his present condition; and it would be a great comfort to our invalid mother to have him brought home so that he can be tenderly nursed until he dies." "My son," said Mr. Lincoln, "I should like to grant your request, but I cannot do it. You don't know what a pressure is brought to bear upon me in such matters. Why, there are senators and members of Congress that would be glad to have their relatives and friends paroled on such terms as you ask, and cannot accomplish it."... Though somewhat disheartened, I again repeated the story of my brother's extreme illness, and the comfort it would be to my mother to have him with her in his dying condition. I said: "Mr. Lincoln, this is a case of life and death. If my brother remains much longer in prison on that bleak, dreary island, exposed to all the severity of an exceptionally cold winter, he cannot last very much longer. You are the only person in the United States that can do absolutely as you please in such matters; and you can release him if you choose to do so, no matter what people say or think."... Finally Mr. Lincoln sank into a state of deep meditation. He sat with his elbows on his knees, his face in his hands, and gazed long and intently into the great wood fire...

Suddenly, without warning, and when, from his long silence, I had concluded my cause was lost, Mr. Lincoln sprang to his feet...and said, as he looked me full in the face, "I'll do it; I'll do it!" Walking over to his desk, he picked up a small paper card case which held visiting-cards such as ladies generally use. Mr. Lincoln held it between his first finger and thumb up to his ear, and shook it to see if there were any cards left. I could distinctly hear the rattle of a single card. Finding what he was looking for, the President sat down, and placing the card before him, wrote very slowly and deliberately. I supposed he was writing an order to some clerk, or to John Hay, to have the parole papers made out. Such was my ignorance of the forms necessary to liberate prisoners that I imagined I should see a large official document with signatures and counter-signatures, seals, etc. Therefore, I was much surprised when Mr. Lincoln arose, and, holding the card between his forefinger and thumb, read it aloud to me as follows:

Allow Lieut. Waller R. Bullock to be paroled and go to his parents in Baltimore, and remain there until well enough to be exchanged.

———⊱◆⊰———

MAJOR GENERAL O. O. Howard, nicknamed "Old Prayer Book," was a Civil War hero, a friend of the president, and the future founder of Howard University in Washington. He wrote down this story about a presidential pardon within a few days of hearing it from his friend, Congressman Daniel J. Morrell, who was president of the Cambria Iron Company of Johnstown, Pennsylvania.

A widow had her only son at work in the Cambria mills, at Johnstown, but he could not resist enlisting, and while the Army of the Potomac lay inactive during the winter months he returned to Johnstown, called there by the need of his old mother for support. He began work in the mills, and being an expert he made several dollars a day, which he gave to his mother, and she saved money every week.

He always told his mother he was going back to the army in the spring whenever it could move. The young man was discovered, arrested and tried as a deserter. So many had deserted that it was resolved to make examples of a few, and he was ordered to be shot.

Mr. Morrell…was visited by the mother and told the story. She begged to be taken to see Mr. Lincoln. Finally Mr. Morrell could resist her entreaties no more and said: "Come to the train tomorrow night and I will take you to Washington, and you will see Mr. Lincoln, if possible, and I will send you home again."

Mr. Morrell was a great favorite with Mr. Lincoln, and when he told him that the mother was in the next room Lincoln said: "Now, Dan, that is not kind of you. You know I ought not to see her; but the son did give all his earnings to his mother, and he was a good boy?"

"Yes, Mr. President, I am sure he did and that he is a good boy and ought not to be shot."

"Well, Dan, I cannot say no to her. Bring her in."

Mr. Lincoln listened to the woman's story, told between sobs, said nothing, but he had been scribbling a few lines with a pencil on a pad of paper, and his first words were:

"Well, he is a good son. He went to save his mother." Then to the mother direct, "I do not think it would do him any good to shoot him, do you?" That question was too much for the mother, and she broke down. Lincoln took the little folded paper and handing it to Morrell said:

"Dan, you go with that direct to the court-martial and deliver it, but mind that neither you nor he is to tell [Secretary of War] Stanton."

When Morrell found the open air he unrolled the crumpled bit of paper and found written:

"Send this boy (giving his name) to his regiment at the front.   *—Abraham Lincoln."*

CONFEDERATE SOLDIER THOMAS THEOPHILUS *Brown was captured by Union soldiers at the battle of Brandy Station, Virginia, in the summer of 1863 and sent to the Old Capitol Prison in Washington. He and his brother, who had been captured with him, were suspected to be spies, a crime punishable by death. When Brown's wife, India Frances Brown, found out her husband might be shot, she resolved to somehow cross the Union lines, make her way to the Old Capitol*

Prison, and prove to the Union authorities that her husband was innocent. Her home of Alexandria was over ten miles from Washington, and she was told that no passes were being issued to allow passage of southern civilians through the lines. But she resolved to try and took her nursing infant and an old servant with her.

She determined that the only way to reach her husband was by rowing across the Potomac River at night, hoping to avoid detection by the sentinels on the Union gunboats. While she anxiously quieted her child, the servant rowed past the gunboats. They passed undetected, and the next day, she managed to make her way to the Capitol Prison, where she was told that she could not visit anyone unless she got a pass from the War Department.

Frightened but resolute to obtain a pardon for her husband, she took her baby and went to see Secretary of War Stanton. This took days, but when she finally had her chance to declare her husband's innocence, he refused to believe her reasons. Infuriated, she angrily said to the gruff old Secretary of War: "General Stanton, you are no gentleman! I shall go to authority higher than you to free my husband!" That meant just one person: Abraham Lincoln. The narrator of the story, who heard it from India Frances Brown's daughter, relates the following:

Exactly how long it took India Frances Brown to get an interview with Abraham Lincoln, her daughter does not recall… On September seventh, however the waiting girl with the child in her arms, was ushered into the presence of Abraham Lincoln. They were left alone and she saw the lean gaunt slightly stooping figure of the President towering over her. She stood speechless for a moment, not believing that she really was there, and then realizing how much depended on her visit her eyes filled with tears. Abraham Lincoln came over to her, smiled and gently put her into a chair.

"What can I do for you?" he asked her and the ordinary words laved her spirit like a breath of spring air.

"It took all fear from her," India Brown's daughter relates. "Mother had been terribly afraid of coming to him. She had heard hard things said about this man, Abraham Lincoln, who had for a 'notion' as she had heard people say, plunged the country into war. But there he was, homely as his pictures had shown him to be, but beautiful in a way that no picture showed. Giving her all the time she wanted, he let Mother tell her story in her own way. Sometimes, Mother said, he smiled and sometimes he just rubbed his chin.

"Mother was crying when she finished. Nelly, who was sitting in Mother's lap, smiled at the President and half to hide his confusion and half to help Mother pull herself together he lifted the baby up in his arms and held her close to his cheeks. To Mother's great amazement she heard Nelly say, 'Papa.' Maybe it was the fact of Lincoln's being a man that made her do it or maybe it was some resemblance. Anyway, Abraham Lincoln laughed. He put the baby back into Mother's lap and walked back and forth a few times. Then he sat down at his desk and wrote something on a sheet of paper. When he finished he reread what he had written and then brought the paper to Mother, saying:

"'Take this to Secretary Stanton, Mrs. Brown. If what you say is true, your husband will be returned to you.'

"One thing more he said before he opened the door for her: 'Mrs. Brown, you are a brave little woman.'

"That was all. The door closed softly behind her before she could pull herself together to thank him."

On winged feet India Frances Brown returned to the office of the War Secretary and presented the communication from the President. This time there was no waiting. Secretary Stanton saw her at once, read the brief message and, as she later told her children, bit his lip and smiled. She felt, she said, "like a person glorified."

The note from President Lincoln, verified by records in the War Department, asked that the cases of Thomas Theophilus and George Emory Brown be investigated. Three days later, on September tenth, the superintendent of the Old Capitol Prison was directed to discharge Thomas Theophilus Brown and George Emory Brown on their taking the oath of allegiance. According to the prison records this was administered on September 9, 1863.

India Frances Brown, needless to say, was at the prison gates on that memorable day.

"When she saw Father, she didn't recognize him," her daughter tells us. "He was thin almost to emaciation, his face was shaggy with a beard, his body was barely covered with the rags he wore and he was trembling with fever and nerves. His feet were torn and scarred. All his life he carried the marks of his last war experience.

"As soon as she could Mother took him home with her to Alexandria where she nursed him back to health. It was not until he was partly himself again that she told him of the great debt of gratitude they owed to Abraham Lincoln. Father, Mother declared, said nothing but only hid his face in the pillows and cried."

CHAPTER FIVE
LINCOLN AND THE SOLDIERS

———◆———

As the years of war dragged on and the soldiers saw their comrades die or be carried away in the wagonloads of wounded, they recognized in the careworn face of their president that he was a casualty of the war too. He had performed numerous formal reviews of the troops on the parade ground during the course of the war, and many noticed that each time they saw him, he looked older, sadder, and more exhausted than the time before.

This caused the invisible chain that bound the soldiers to their president to become ever stronger, and by the end of the war, it was one that could not be broken. When things went wrong or bloody battles were lost, the men blamed anything or anyone else but not their beloved commander in chief.

One private in the Army of the Potomac spoke for many of his comrades when he said that "we have learned to love him as well as he appears to love his boys in blue, and we all would be willing to sacrifice anything for such a man."

Another soldier from the famous Iron Brigade—one of the toughest units in the army—said that "he is the man to suit the soldiers." Many of the men carried small photos of the president in their knapsacks and referred to him affectionately as "Father Abraham," "Honest Abe," or "Uncle Abe." They believed Lincoln was an honest and faithful leader who had their interests—as well as those of the nation—foremost in his heart.

Abraham Lincoln had the highest respect for the soldiers. He made it a point to publicly praise, encourage, and thank them at every opportune moment. An example of his praise was what he said to the audience at a hospital fund-raiser in Philadelphia: "Say what you will, after all the most is due to the soldier, who takes his life in his hands and goes to fight the battles of his country." At another fund-raiser he said, "This extraordinary war in which we are engaged falls heavily upon all classes of people, but the most heavily upon the soldier. For it has been said, all that a man hath will he give for his life; and while all contribute of their substance the soldier puts his life at stake, and often yields it up in his country's cause. The highest merit, then, is due to the soldier."

Lincoln never missed an opportunity to deflect praise from himself to the troops. During the occasion of a serenade that was intended to honor him for issuing the Emancipation

Proclamation, he told his admirers that his difficulties were "scarcely so great as the difficulties of those who, upon the battle field, are endeavoring to purchase with their blood and their lives the future happiness and prosperity of this country." He concluded by asking the spectators to shout three cheers for the men and officers of the army.

Lincoln considered the lowliest private his equal and told one visiting diplomat from Europe that "with us every soldier is a man of character and must be treated with more consideration than is customary in Europe." Early in the war, when he first began visiting the army in their encampments around Washington, he told the men that if they ever had a problem that could not be solved or ever felt themselves ill-used, they could come to him personally for the remedy. Many did just that. One historian has estimated that, between Lincoln's conversations with soldiers in the field and their meetings with him in the White House, the president had personal interviews with at least two thousand soldiers during the war.[8] Those two thousand interviews were not limited to Union soldiers. When Lincoln visited the hospitals, he extended as much kindness and sympathy to the soldiers dressed in gray as he did those who were dressed in blue.

The soldiers had innumerable problems, and Lincoln did his best to solve as many as he could. Their troubles

---

8   Estimate is from Carwardine, *Lincoln: Profiles in Power*, 65.

ranged all the way from the small ones, such as requests for furlough, to the monumental, such as clemency from courts-martial. If a soldier complained he hadn't received his back pay, Lincoln would assign an aide to look into the cause and required him to report back on what he found. When a man thought he had been unfairly treated by his officers, Lincoln contacted the War Department and asked for a review of the case. When a sixteen-year-old boy asked for promotion from private to captain, Lincoln spoke to the young man as a father would to a son and convinced him it would be best for him to go back and earn his promotion in the field.

Lincoln's secretaries John G. Nicolay and John Hay always noticed the president's caring demeanor when talking to soldiers. In late April 1861, Hay wrote that "the wounded soldiers of the Sixth Massachusetts, including several officers, came to pay a visit to the President. They were a little shy when they entered the room—having the traditional New England awe of authorities and rulers. Lincoln received them with sympathetic kindness which put them at ease after the interchange of the first greetings. His words of sincere thanks for their patriotism and their suffering, his warm praise of their courage, his hearty recognition of their great service to the public, and his earnestly expressed confidence in their further devotion, quickly won their trust."

Most soldiers encountered Lincoln during troop reviews

in the field. It was customary for him to ride horseback past the troops while they stood in formation. Colonel Horace Porter recalled one review: "Mr. Lincoln wore a very high black silk hat and black trousers and frockcoat. Like most men who had been brought up in the West, he had good command of a horse, but it must be acknowledged that in appearance he was not a very dashing rider. On this occasion, by the time he had reached the troops he was completely covered with dust, and the black color of his clothes had changed to Confederate gray. As he had no straps, his trousers gradually worked up above his ankles, and gave him the appearance of a country farmer riding into town wearing his Sunday clothes. A citizen on horseback is always an odd sight in the midst of a uniformed army, and the picture presented by the President bordered upon the grotesque. However, the troops were so lost in admiration of the man that the humorous aspect did not seem to strike them. The soldiers rapidly passed the word along the line that 'Uncle Abe' had joined them, and cheers broke forth from all the commands, and enthusiastic shouts and even words of familiar greeting met him on all sides."

Another soldier recalled that Lincoln's tall hat and ungainly form "presented a very comical picture, calculated to provoke laughter along the entire length of the lines." Yet they did not laugh. One soldier explained that it was because of "that sad, anxious face, so full of melancholy foreboding, that peered forth from his shaggy eyebrows." They perceived that he looked careworn and anxious and that there must have been a "heap of trouble on the old man's mind."

Many soldiers wrote home and talked about the president's saddened appearance. Some saw tears in his eyes, which caused them to ponder his difficulties as the nation's leader during the war. One soldier's letter revealed that each time he saw the president, "the lines of care upon his kindly face grew deeper." Another lamented, "Poor man, I pity him, and almost wonder at his being alive. The gigantic work upon his hands, and the task upon his physical frame, must be very great."

Lincoln's awkward manner, homely face, sad eyes, and warm smile endeared him to the men, and they could not restrain themselves from cheering him "to the echo." Although the soldiers of the Army of the Potomac also cheered their commander, General George B. McClellan, one New York soldier said that McClellan's popularity with the army "will never measure 1/100th part of Honest Abe's. Such cheers as greeted [the president] never tickled the ears of Napoleon in his palmist days."

A sergeant from Massachusetts reported that he "could easily perceive why and how the president was called 'Honest Abe'… I think his coming down, or up, to see us done us all good." Another soldier wrote, "We marched proudly away, for we all felt proud to know that we had been permitted to see and salute him." "What a depth of devotion, sympathy, and reassurance were conveyed through his smile," recalled a Wisconsin soldier. "How our hearts went out to him. We knew that 'Old Abe'—as he was called by the people who loved him, trusted him—was true."

Ultimately, the troops were able to do much more for Lincoln than cheer him. When it came time for the presidential election of 1864 and their other favorite, former General George B. McClellan, was running against Lincoln as the Democratic candidate, nearly eighty percent of the soldier vote went for Lincoln.[9] As the following stories show, there was a strong affection, born of mutual respect, between the soldiers and their president.

LINCOLN BELIEVED THAT "A private soldier has as much right to justice as a major general," and his many actions were a result of an effort on his part to see that all soldiers were treated equally. Lincoln's close friend, journalist Noah Brooks, described one of Lincoln's visits with a group of soldiers in the White House.

9   See chapter eight of Davis, *Lincoln's Men*, for a complete analysis of the soldier vote in 1864.

Mr. Lincoln's manner toward enlisted men, with whom he occasionally met and talked, was always delightful in its bonhomie and its absolute freedom from anything like condescension... One day in the latter part of March, 1863, I was at the White House with the President, and he told me to tarry for a while, as a party of Ohio soldiers who had been lately exchanged after many harassing experiences were coming to see him. It appeared that these were the survivors of what was then known as the Marietta raid. Twenty-one men from Ohio regiments of the command of General O. M. Mitchel, then in northern Alabama, were sent on a dangerous mission to destroy the railroad communications of Chattanooga to the south and east. The expedition failed, and of the original number only six returned to Washington, after incredible hardships and suffering—one third of the party having escaped, and another fraction having been hanged as spies, the rebel authorities deciding that the fact that these men wore citizen's clothes within an enemy's lines put them in that category.

The men, who were introduced to the President by General E. A. Hitchcock, then on duty in Washington, were Mason, Parrott, Pittenger,

Buffum, Reddick, and Bensinger. Their names were given to the President, and, without missing the identity of a single man, he shook hands all round with an unaffected cordiality and good-fellowship difficult to describe. He had heard their story in all its details, and as he talked with each, asking questions and making his shrewd comments on what they had to say, it was evident that for the moment this interesting interview was to him of supreme importance... The stories of these long-suffering men, and the cheerful lightness with which they narrated their courageous and hazardous deeds, impressed Mr. Lincoln very deeply. Speaking of the men afterward, he said, with much feeling, that their bearing, and their apparent unconsciousness of having taken their lives in their hands, with the chances of death all against them, presented an example of the apparent disregard of the tremendous issues of life and death which was so strong a characteristic of the American soldier.

Sixteen-year-old Thomas S. Hopkins wanted to enlist immediately when the Civil War broke out in 1861, but his parents would not allow it. He persisted in his appeals until his mother finally relented in June 1862, and he joined the army. Hopkins, who was in many bloody battles in the war, describes his first glimpse of the president.

My first view of Mr. Lincoln was soon after the battle of Antietam, in the fall of 1862. Mr. Lincoln had come to review the Army of the Potomac. Our regiment had marched a long distance in the early morning to reach the reviewing field and then came a long, long wait. I was tired, hungry, and thirsty. But finally there came the sound of bugles and loud cries of "Attention!" from officers. A cloud of dust

swept toward us from far down the line, and out of it gradually emerged a great number of field and staff-officers, their horses galloping rapidly. At the head rode Major General George B. McClellan, and at his side a civilian, dressed in black and wearing a high silk hat. The contrast between the latter and those who were attired in all the glittering panoply of war was striking. In the passing glimpse that I obtained, about all that could be observed was that Mr. Lincoln was very tall and-rode his horse with wonderful ease. But in the fraction of the moment that my eyes rested on Mr. Lincoln, somehow my heart warmed toward the great man, and I whispered softly to myself: "I'm glad I enlisted!"

ASSISTANT ATTORNEY GENERAL TITIAN J. Coffey provided valuable counsel to Lincoln during his first term of office and was instrumental in the ruling that gave black soldiers equivalent pay with white soldiers. Coffey recalled Lincoln's act of kindness toward a young soldier's wife in the spring of 1863. It was this sort of magnanimity by Lincoln that endeared him to the soldiers.

A very handsome and attractive young lady from Philadelphia came to my office with a note from a friend, asking me to assist her in obtaining an interview with the President. Some time before she had been married to a young man who was a lieutenant in a Pennsylvania regiment. He had been compelled to leave her the day after the wedding to rejoin his command in the Army of the Potomac. After some time he obtained leave of absence, returned to Philadelphia, and started on a brief honeymoon journey with his bride. A movement of the army being imminent, the War Department issued a peremptory order requiring all absent officers to rejoin their regiments by a certain day on penalty of dismissal in case of disobedience. The bride and groom, away on their hurried wedding tour, failed to see the order, and on their return he was met by a notice of his dismissal from the service. The young fellow was completely prostrated by the disgrace, and his wife hurried to Washington to get him restored. I obtained for her an interview with the President. She told her story with simple and pathetic eloquence, and wound up by saying:

"Mr. Lincoln, won't you help us? I promise you, if you will restore him, he will be faithful to his duty."

The President had listened to her with evident

sympathy, and a half-amused smile at her earnestness, and as she closed her appeal he said with parental kindness:

"And you say, my child, that Fred was compelled to leave you the day after the wedding? Poor fellow, I don't wonder at his anxiety to get back, and if he stayed a little longer than he ought to have done we'll have to overlook his fault this time. Take this card to the Secretary of War and he will restore your husband."

She went to the War Department, saw the Secretary, who rebuked her for troubling the President, and dismissed her somewhat curtly. As it happened, on her way down the War Department stairs, her hopes chilled by the Secretary's abrupt manner, she met the President ascending. He recognized her, and with a pleasant smile said:

"Well, my dear, have you seen the Secretary?"

"Yes, Mr. Lincoln," she replied, "and he seemed very angry with me for going to you. Won't you speak to him for me?"

"Give yourself no trouble," said he. "I will see that the order is issued."

And in a few days her husband was remanded to his regiment. I am sorry to add that, not long after,

he was killed at the battle of Gettysburg, thus sealing
with his blood her pledge that he should be faithful
to his duty.

*Lincoln was especially attentive to wounded soldiers when
they came to the White House. Francis Bicknell Carpenter recalled
an incident in a White House receiving line where the president and
Mrs. Lincoln had spent hours greeting military, political, and other
important visitors. The press of the crowd had been so extreme that
the president, thinking of the strain the constant hand-shaking had
on his wife, decided they would dispense with physical contact and
instead offer each visitor a verbal greeting and polite bow.*

The President had been standing for some time,
bowing his acknowledgments to the thronging multitude, when his eye fell upon a couple who had
entered unobserved—a wounded soldier, and his
plainly dressed mother. Before they could pass out,
he made his way to where they stood, and, taking
each of them by the hand, with a delicacy and cordiality which brought tears to many eyes, he assured
them of his interest and welcome. Governors, senators, diplomats, passed with simply a nod; but that
pale young face he might never see again. To him,

and to others like him, did the nation owe its life; and Abraham Lincoln was not the man to forget this, even in the crowded and brilliant assembly of the distinguished of the land.

———◆◆◆———

During the hot summer months, President Lincoln and his family spent their nights at the Soldiers' Home, a place for disabled and retired soldiers, in the northern part of the city. It was somewhat cooler there and provided a respite from the constant demands on his time in the White House. When he traveled back and forth, Lincoln's carriage was usually escorted by a squad of cavalry. One of these cavalrymen, noncommissioned officer Henry W. Knight, wrote of a wonderful deed Lincoln did for a disabled soldier.[10]

I was detailed on one occasion to escort the President to the [Soldiers'] Home. While on our way we had to pass Carver Hospital. As we approached the front gate, I noticed what seemed

---

10 Henry W. Knight frequently guarded the president during the war. His last and most solemn duty as bodyguard for Abraham Lincoln would be to help clear a pathway through the crowds as the mortally wounded president was being carried through the street from Ford's Theatre to the Petersen house, where he died the following day.

to be a young man groping his way, as if he were blind, across the road. Hearing the carriage and horses approaching, he became frightened, and walked in the direction of the approaching danger. Mr. Lincoln quickly observed this and shouted to the coachman to rein in his horses, which he did as they were about to run over the unfortunate youth. I shall never forget the expression of Mr. Lincoln's face on this occasion. Standing beside the carriage was a young man, dressed in the uniform of a private soldier. He had been shot through the left side of the upper part of the face, and the ball, passing from one side to the other, had put out both of his eyes. He could not have been over sixteen or seventeen years of age, and, aside from his blindness, he had a very beautiful face. Mr. Lincoln extended his hand to him, and while he held it he asked him, with a voice trembling with emotion, his name, his regiment and where he lived. The young man answered these questions, and stated that he lived in Michigan; and then Mr. Lincoln made himself known to the blind soldier, and with a look that was a benediction in itself spoke to him a few words of sympathy and bade him good-by. A few days after this incident, an old "chum" from my own regiment wrote me that he was at Carver Hospital, and asked me to come and see him. I went, and while there I asked after the blind soldier who had lost his eyes. I then learned that the following day, after his interview with the President he received a commission as a First Lieutenant in the Regular Army of the United States, accompanied by an order of retirement upon full pay.[11]

<hr />

LINCOLN WAS ALWAYS TERRIBLY affected by the suffering of wounded soldiers. He and Mary would frequently visit Washington's military hospitals, and he would spend hours walking slowly from one hospital bed to another, shaking hands and offering words of thanks and encouragement. Mary would frequently bring treats for the men such as flowers or baskets of fruit. She would sometimes sit and write letters for the soldiers as they dictated words that were, for many, their last communication to their families.

One nurse, Amandsa Akin Stearns, in her book The Lady Nurse of Ward E, *wrote about the president's visits to the Armory Square Hospital in Washington.*

He came often to visit the hospital and shake hands

<hr />

11 Per Albert Nofi, *A Civil War Treasury*, a first lieutenant's pay was $105.50 per month, as opposed to a private's pay of $13 per month.

with the soldiers, always with a kind word, when his eyes had a sad, far-away look, and he often paused before those suffering most intensely to utter a warm "God bless you."... It was pathetic to see him pass from bed to bed and give each occupant the warm, honest grasp for which he is noted... His homely face with such sad eyes and ungainly figure did not fill my youthful idea of a "President of the United States"; but it was a grand thing for him to come and cheer our soldier boys with his presence.

MORE THAN ONE HOSPITAL attendant noticed how deeply Lincoln was touched by the suffering of the wounded soldiers. Union officer William E. Doster recalled the following story.

In my daily inspections of the guards at the hospitals at Washington, I often met the President, quietly going through the wards, giving a kind word to one, and a cheerful message to another, and it was impossible not to be convinced that the suffering and tragedies of this great struggle touched a tender chord in his nature, and that he felt deeply the crippling and slaughter of so many fine young men, the disease, bereavements, funerals, and mourning on both sides, very much as an affectionate father would feel that in his own family.

IN ADDITION TO THE hospitals in Washington, Lincoln also visited the army's field hospitals, and he often greeted both Union and Confederate wounded. After the Battle of Antietam in September 1862, a fight that resulted in the highest number of casualties for any single-day battle during the war, Lincoln visited the Army of the Potomac in western Maryland. While there, the president looked over the battlefields and reviewed the troops. He also went to a hospital the Union army had established for wounded Confederate soldiers in Sharpsburg, Maryland, which resulted in this remarkable scene, chronicled by a Baltimore newspaperman in the Sacramento Daily Union.

Passing through one of the hospitals devoted exclusively to Confederate sick and wounded, President Lincoln's attention was drawn to a young Georgian—a fine noble looking youth—stretched upon a humble cot. He was pale, emaciated and anxious, far from kindred and home, vibrating, as it were, between life and death. Every stranger that entered [was] caught in his restless eyes, in hope of their being some relative or friend. President Lincoln observed this youthful soldier, approached and spoke, asking him if he suffered much pain. "I do," was the reply. "I have lost a leg, and feel I am sinking from exhaustion." "Would you," said Mr. Lincoln, "shake hands with me if I were to tell you who I am?" The response was affirmative. "There should," remarked the young Georgian, "be no enemies in this place." Then, said the distinguished visitor, "I am Abraham Lincoln, President of the United States." The young sufferer raised his head, looking amazed, and freely extended his hand, which Mr. Lincoln took and pressed tenderly for some time. There followed an instinctive pause. The wounded Confederate's eyes melted into tears, his lips quivered, and his heart beat full. President Lincoln bent over him motionless and dumb. His eyes, too, were overflowing, thus giving utterance to emotions far beyond the power of any language to describe. It was a most touching scene. Not a dry eye was present. Silence was subsequently broken by a kind conciliatory conversation between the President and his young Confederate, when they parted, there being but slim hope for the latter's recovery.

ANOTHER EXAMPLE OF LINCOLN'S kindness toward Confederate wounded was an incident that took place after he had been in a hospital all day with a company of friends. Dr. Francis Durbin Blakeslee, related the following story.

Just as they were entering their carriages to leave, an attendant rushed out and said to one of the party: "There is a Confederate prisoner in one of the wards that the President did not visit, and he wants to see the President." When Lincoln was told, he said, "I'll go back." As he approached the cot and extended his hand, the young fellow exclaimed: "I knew they were mistaken! I knew they were mistaken!" He had heard all that talk about the ape, the baboon, the gorilla; but one glance at the kindly face dispelled it all and he said: "I knew they were mistaken!"

"What can I do for you, young man?" inquired Lincoln. "O, I don't know anybody up here, and the surgeon tells me I can't live, and I wanted to see you before I die." The President asked him about his father, mother, his brothers and his sisters. The young fellow's confidence was won, and he told about his family and his home; about his keepsakes and what he wanted done with them. Lincoln listened sympathetically and promised to see that a letter was written. He still tarried, trying to prepare the young man for "the great adventure." Presently he said: "Now, my boy, I have been here nearly all day. I am a very busy man and I ought to be going; but is there anything more that I can do for you?" "I was hoping you would stay and see me through." And the great tears rolled down on Lincoln's coat-sleeve as he continued to minister to the dying boy.

THE LAST VISIT LINCOLN *ever made to a military hospital was on the Monday before the assassination. When the president was returning from Richmond, he stopped at Union Army headquarters at City Point, Virginia. Calling upon the head surgeon at that place, Lincoln told him that he wished to visit all the hospitals under his charge and shake hands with every soldier.*

The surgeon asked if he knew what he was undertaking, there being five or six thousand soldiers at that place, and it would be quite a tax upon his strength to visit all the wards and shake hands with every soldier. Mr. Lincoln answered with a smile, he "guessed he was equal to the task; at any rate he would try, and go as far as he could; he should never, probably, see the boys again, and he wanted them to know that he appreciated what they had done for their country."

Finding it useless to try to dissuade him, the surgeon began his rounds with the President, who walked from bed to bed, extending his hand to all, saying a few words of sympathy to some, making kind inquiries of others, and welcomed by all with the heartiest cordiality.

As they passed along, they came to a ward in which lay a Rebel who had been wounded and was a prisoner. As the tall figure of the kindly visitor appeared in sight he was recognized by the Rebel soldier, who, raising himself on his elbow in bed, watched Mr. Lincoln as he approached, and extending his hand exclaimed, while tears ran down his cheeks: "Mr. Lincoln, I have long wanted to see you, to ask your forgiveness for ever raising my hand against the old flag." Mr. Lincoln was moved to tears. He heartily shook the hand of the repentant Rebel, and assured him of his good-will, and with a few words of kind advice passed on.

After some hours the tour of the various hospitals

was made, and Mr. Lincoln returned with the surgeon to his office. They had scarcely entered, however, when a messenger came saying that one ward had been omitted, and "the boys" wanted to see the President. The surgeon, who was thoroughly tired, and knew Mr. Lincoln must be, tried to dissuade him from going; but the good man said he must go back; he would not knowingly omit one, 'the boys' would be so disappointed. So he went with the messenger, accompanied by the surgeon, and shook hands with the gratified soldiers, and then returned again to the office.

The surgeon expressed the fear that the President's arm would be lamed with so much hand-shaking, saying that it certainly must ache. Mr. Lincoln smiled, and saying something about his "strong muscles," stepped out at the open door, took up a very large, heavy axe which lay there by a log of wood, and chopped vigorously for a few moments, sending the chips flying in all directions; and then, pausing, he extended his right arm to its full length, holding the axe out horizontally, without its even quivering as he held it. Strong men who looked on—men accustomed to manual labor—could not hold the same axe in that position for a moment. Returning to the office, he took a glass of lemonade, for he would take no stronger beverage; and while he was within, the chips he had chopped were gathered up and safely cared for by a hospital steward, because they were "the chips that Father Abraham chopped." In a few hours more the beloved President was at home in Washington.

POSTSCRIPT
A LEGACY FOR ALL

THE END OF ABRAHAM Lincoln's life story is familiar to all. Five days after the principal Confederate army under General Robert E. Lee surrendered, a well-known Shakespearean actor, John Wilkes Booth, entered the presidential box at Ford's Theatre and shot the nation's sixteenth president while he and his wife were watching a play. Lincoln died the following morning, on April 15, 1865, and the nation was plunged into deep mourning for the loss of the simple prairie lawyer who had become the most esteemed man of his age.

Flags hung at half mast, countless buildings were draped in black, eulogies were preached in thousands of pulpits across the land, and Lincoln's casket was transported slowly by funeral train back to the place of his internment in Springfield, Illinois. Millions of people watched the train pass by on its roundabout journey home. They waited alongside the railroad tracks, in towns and fields, in rain and sun—all for the purpose of honoring him.

Lincoln's life exemplified what is now known as the American dream. Born into poverty, deprived of formal education, and beginning as a common laborer, he improved himself through the study of books and social interaction with his neighbors. Finally, he became the president who led the nation through its greatest crisis.

But these accomplishments alone were not the fulfillment of the dream. Equally as important as his intellectual and social improvement was his moral self-development. He rose above his society's prejudices regarding racial equality.[12] He became the servant leader, the transforming leader, who inspired millions of Americans to sacrifice their own well-being for the benefit of others and for future generations.

Lincoln's religious faith increased significantly during the war, and when his old friend Joshua Speed admitted to him that he was still a skeptic,[13] the President replied,

---

12   Up until Lincoln was president, he was not a vocal proponent of complete equality of the races. But by the war's end, he was a proponent of giving black men, particularly the soldiers and the educated, the right to vote. It was this proposal by Lincoln that inspired John Wilkes Booth to assassinate him.

13   Many scholars attest that both Speed and Lincoln had been religious skeptics when young men, but Lincoln had become much more religious in his later years. When President, he prayed and read the Bible almost daily. See Wayne C. Temple, *Abraham Lincoln: From Skeptic to Prophet*, for discussion of Lincoln's faith.

"You are wrong, Speed. Take all of this book [the Bible] upon reason that you can and the balance on faith, and you will live and die a happier and better man." Lincoln's close friend Noah Brooks said the president "was a praying man, and daily sought from God that aid which he had long since learned man could not give him." As president, Lincoln questioned God's purpose for the great conflict he was leading, but instead of becoming despondent over the casualties, he finally arrived at a place of peace with "the Almighty," whom he concluded had "His own purposes" in the war.

Six weeks before he died, Abraham Lincoln stood on a podium high above his countrymen and spoke these final words of his second inaugural address: "With malice toward none; with charity for all; with firmness in the right, as God gives us to see the right, let us strive on to finish the work we are in; to bind up the nation's wounds; to care for him who shall have borne the battle, and for his widow, and his orphan—to do all which may achieve and cherish a just, and a lasting peace, among ourselves, and with all nations."

FORMER SLAVE NANCY BUSHROD lived with her three children in Washington. Her husband Tom was in the Union Army, and since

Nancy had been unable to find employment, his private's salary of $13 per month was all she had to live on. For some reason, the money stopped coming, so on April 14, 1865, Nancy decided to ask the President of the United States for help and walked five miles to the White House. Lincoln's words to her that day changed not only Nancy Bushrod's life but the lives of her children and grandchildren as well.

The fact that she was one of the last visitors to see Lincoln that day is corroborated in reliable sources, and the narrative below was published by Esther May Carter of Oneida, Kentucky, who heard the story from a woman named Harriet who knew Nancy Bushrod.[14]

One morning the children cried because they were hungry, and Nancy's mind snapped into resolve. She would see the President himself and ask him to help her get Tom's pay. Tom was fighting for the Union, and the Union would help her find food for Tom's children; and to Nancy's simple mind the Union was—Abraham Lincoln.

She hadn't touched food for two days and was faint from her five-mile walk when she reached the White House. "Business with the President?" the guards at the gate asked, in good humor. Her answer was grim: "Before God, yes."

---

14 The original dialects of Nancy Bushrod and local policeman Sandy McVean have been updated to contemporary English for clarity.

"Let her pass—they'll stop her farther on," she heard one guard say, so she took a deep breath and went on. The guard at the main entrance stopped her: "No further, madam. Against orders." But in a flash she darted under his arm and went straight to the guard at the farther door.

"For God's sake, please let me see Mr. Lincoln!"

"Madam, the President is busy; he can not see you."

At this Nancy must have given a little cry, for, in her own words, "All of a sudden the door opened, and Mr. Lincoln himself stood lookin' at me. I knew it was him, for there was a whimsy smile on his blessed face, and he was sayin', deep and soft like, 'There is time for all who need me. Let the good woman come in.'"…

He heard her story through, then said: "You are entitled to your soldier-husband's pay. Come this time to-morrow, and the papers will be signed and ready for you." Then, as she turned to leave…he called her back:

"My good woman, perhaps you'll see many a day when all the food in the house is a single loaf of bread. Even so, give every child a slice, and send your children off to school."

With that, the President bowed—"like I was a

natural-born lady," Nancy always tells it, and turned to a table piled high with work.

All the long walk back, in drizzling rain, Lincoln's kindness enveloped her like sunshine, and the words, "Send your children off to school," crystallized into purpose.

But there was no reaching the President the following day. That very night the fatal shot was fired that plunged a nation into grief, and the next morning gave Lincoln "to the ages."... Nancy couldn't get near the White House that next morning, for the crowds that blocked Pennsylvania Avenue. It was a big Scotch policeman, blinking back the tears, who told her, in his bluff, kind way: "You didn't know the President's dead? Woman, whaur ye livin?"

Nancy clung to the nearest post for support—her small world seemed shot to pieces—then she straightened:

"Before God I swear it, I'm going to find work, I'm going to make Mr. Lincoln's words come true. I'm going to send my children off to school!"... Sandy McVean, the big policeman who heard her cry out over Lincoln's death, got her a janitress job in Ford's Theater... [and later] Nancy, with the children's help, ran a Snow-flake Home

President Abraham Lincoln: 1865

Laundry that was the talk of the town. And out of the grades into high school climbed the three children, the twin boys talking college all the time—and meaning it...

"And now," Harriet [the narrator] concluded, "not a mother among us has more reason to be proud of her children than Nancy Bushrod. Her David is pastor of the First Colored Church in Detroit; her

Booker is teaching at Tuskegee (he was Booker T. Washington's own 'find' on one of his lecture tours), and her [granddaughter] Beulah was…valedictorian of her class last June and now taking college work in expression.…" Esther May Carter concluded her story with the following note about eighty year-old Nancy Bushrod: "It's the glory of her life that she knew him, and no one chats with her who doesn't hear: 'Honey, I knew Lincoln—an' I know him to-day—an' I'll know him yonder, when Sweet Chariot Swings Low for me.'"

ACKNOWLEDGMENTS

I<small>T HAS BEEN MY</small> privilege to be a board member of the Abraham Lincoln Institute (ALI) since 1999, serving as that organization's webmaster. Most of the ALI's board of directors are nationally recognized experts on the subject of Abraham Lincoln, and two of them were kind enough to take time out of their incredibly busy schedules to review the *Conversations with Lincoln* manuscript and offer constructive criticism. These scholars are:

William C. Harris, the author of a dozen celebrated Lincoln books and professor emeritus of history from North Carolina State University. Professor Harris has written some of the most widely acclaimed Lincoln books of our age, including *Lincoln and the Border States: Preserving the Union* (2011) and *Lincoln's Last Months* (2004). Professor Harris is also author of the upcoming *Lincoln and Congress*, a contribution to the Concise Lincoln Library, to be published by the Southern Illinois University Press.

Joan E. Cashin, professor of history at Ohio State University. Professor Cashin is the former chair of the board of the Abraham Lincoln Institute and author of *First Lady of the Confederacy: Varina Davis's Civil War* (2006), which was the winner of the 2008 Fletcher Pratt Award.

To both scholars, I offer a sincere thank-you.

I would also like to extend my thanks to the amazing team at Sourcebooks. Although I cannot recognize everyone, I would at least like to acknowledge the wonderful editorial staff, beginning with Stephanie Bowen, Grace Menary-Winefield, and Cassie Gutman, along with Sabrina Baskey and Barbara Hower.

And as always, my deepest thanks go to Jean, my wife and best friend for over thirty-six years. She has put up with stacks of Lincoln books in every room of the house, listened to my interminable Lincoln stories, and patiently read and edited the manuscript multiple times. All of this has been done faithfully and cheerfully, in spite of the fact that the list of honey-dos grows ever longer.

A NOTE ON SOURCES

ALTHOUGH MANY OF THE stories in this book include people who are rarely heard from in Lincoln biographies, the majority of the sources for these anecdotes are familiar to Lincoln scholars.

The fact that many of these stories were first printed in the nineteenth century and some of them have been out of print for decades presents its own set of challenges. Original misspellings and punctuation were left unchanged unless they made the story unclear. When there was only one witness for the details of a conversation, such as with former slave Nancy Bushrod's interview with Lincoln, it was necessary to carefully consider the reliability of the source or search for corroborating evidence that a conversation did in fact take place. Sometimes, as in the case of Nancy Bushrod, corroboration was easily found in dependable resources such as Earl S. Miers's *Lincoln Day by Day*.

Ultimately, scholars know that the decision about

which Lincoln anecdotes to include in a book comes down to the author's best judgment. With that in mind, this student of history has made a sincere effort to put together a credible collection of Lincoln stories that reflect the honorable nature of our nation's greatest leader.

NOTES

PREFACE

xi   "and cannot change" Burlingame, *Abraham Lincoln: A Life*, 2:493.

xii   "relations to recommend" Basler, *Collected Works*, 1:9.

INTRODUCTION

xiii   "Bright and early…the story of a little girl" Wilson, *Intimate Memories of Lincoln*, 543–547.

CHAPTER 1

1   "raised to farm work" Wilson, *Honor's Voice*, 86.

2   "esteemed of my fellow men" Basler, *Collected Works*, 1:9.

4   "had in Illinois" Burlingame, *Abraham Lincoln: A Life*, 1:316.

6   "always hated slavery" Basler, *Collected Works*, 2:492.

10   "When he…and he did" Whitney, *Life on the Circuit*, 33.

11   "Mr. Lincoln had…to take part" Wilson, *Intimate Memories of Lincoln*, 27.

14   "I [William] first…in battle array" Jayne, *Abraham Lincoln: Personal Reminiscences of the Martyred President*, 16–17.

16   "He had ridden…I'm moved!" Browne, *Every-day Life of Abraham Lincoln*, 151–153.

17   "shout for joy" Hertz, *Lincoln Talks*, 114–115.

18   "I lived…willingly missed another" Stevens, *A Reporter's Lincoln*, 63.

19   "I made a visit…truthfulness of Abraham Lincoln" Stevens, *A Reporter's Lincoln*, 66–67.

23   "All at once…fail to join in it" Schurz, *Reminiscences of Carl Schurz*, 2:90–91.

26   "He took…of the race" Wilson, *Lincoln Among His Friends*, 120–121.

28   "When Lincoln was…institution of slavery" Wilson, *Intimate Memories of Lincoln*, 175.

29   "One day…need be no war" Browne, *Every-day Life of Abraham Lincoln*, 352–353.

CHAPTER 2

33   "of his statesmanship" Nevins, *Diary of the Civil War*, 28.

34   "re-adopt the Declaration" Basler, *Collected Works*, 2:275.

34   "registered in heaven" Basler, *Collected Works*, 4:261.

36   "what he was saying" Wilson, *Intimate Memories of Lincoln*, 72.

36   "safety in his atmosphere" Rice, *Reminiscences of Abraham Lincoln* 195.

36   "cherished memories of my life" Stanton, "Abraham Lincoln: Personal Memories," 34.

37   "one of the company" Mitgang, *Spectator of America*, 92.

37   "he very much disliked" Whitney, *Life on the Circuit*, 53.

37   "his freest moments" Rice, *Reminiscences of Abraham Lincoln*, 365.

37   "other than respectful" Rice, *Reminiscences of Abraham Lincoln*, 493.

38   "his easiest conversation" Thayer, *Life and Letters of John Hay*, 188–191.

38   "There I saw...that of beauty" Stanton, "Abraham Lincoln: Personal Memories," 34–37.

43   "Startled to find...swerving or bias" Oldroyd, *Lincoln Memorial: Album-immortelles*, 413–414.

44   "Breakfast over...of his character" Burlingame, *Lincoln Observed*, 84–85.

46   "I see…the Nineteenth Century" Rice, *Reminiscences of Abraham Lincoln*, 469–475.

48   "By and by…in his place" Wilson, *Intimate Memories of Lincoln*, 464–467.

51   "Soon afterwards…or puritan spirit" Russell, *My Diary North and South*, 1:54–55.

53   "Presently I…citizen of the Republic" Carpenter, *Six Months at the White House*, 351–352.

55   "During the…tyrant and usurper" Carpenter, *Six Months at the White House*, 30–31.

56   "Never did I…been their father" Stimmel, *Personal Reminiscences of Abraham Lincoln*, 96.

CHAPTER 3

59   "public opinion baths" Thomas, *Abraham Lincoln*, 462.

59   "our whole people" Holzer, *Dear Mr. Lincoln*, 3.

60   "I *must* see them" Fehrenbacher and Fehrenbacher, *Recollected Words of Abraham Lincoln*, 498.

60   "too poor to be received" Neill, *Reminiscences of the Last Year*, 7.

61   "As his sympathy…himself" Schurz, *Abraham Lincoln: An Essay*, vol. 1, 33–34.

62   "without crying" Carpenter, *Six Months at the White House*, 30.

62   "I was waiting...this great nation" Carpenter, *Six Months at the White House*, 321–322.

65   "I shall never...with the recruiting" Douglass, *Life and Times*, 302–304.

68   "on his shoulder" Rice, *Reminiscences of Abraham Lincoln*, 195.

68   "Among a...person of the President" Carpenter, *Six Months at the White House*, 319–320.

71   "In no other...to say any more" Stoddard, *Inside the White House*, 90–92.

74   "We ascended...in this case" Rice, *Reminiscences of Abraham Lincoln*, 358–360.

77   "Lincoln said...to his regiment" Bates, *Lincoln in the Telegraph Office*, 248–249.

79   "It was about... May God assist me" Holzer, *Lincoln as I Knew Him*, 199–201.

82   "I certainly felt...gets home to her" Wilson, *Lincoln Among His Friends*, 374–378.

CHAPTER 4

87   "away with him" Rice, *Reminiscences of Abraham Lincoln*, 343.

87   "dead than living" Whipple, *Story Life of Abraham Lincoln*, 562.

88   "I won't do it" Lamon, *Recollections of Abraham Lincoln*, 103.

88   "cruelty were shown" Thayer, *Life and Letters of John Hay*, 1:196.

89   "once badly wounded" Nicolay, *Personal Traits of Abraham Lincoln*, 283.

89   "shall be pardoned" Nicolay, *Personal Traits of Abraham Lincoln*, 283.

89   "a weeping child" Hubbard, *Lincoln Reshapes the Presidency*, 103–104.

89   "family and friends" Colfax, *Life and Principles of Abraham Lincoln*, 18.

90   "As he [Ford]...pardon your brother" Carpenter, *Six Months at the White House*, 296–298.

94   "[New York Congressman]...this night's work" Lamon, *Recollections of Abraham Lincoln*, 86–87.

95   "A poor woman...the baby that did it" Carpenter, *Six Months at the White House*, 132–133.

97   "The last interview...a flower would grow" Herndon and Weik, *Herndon's Lincoln*, 2:235–238.

101   "A story my...in the army" Ward, *Abraham Lincoln: Tributes*, 155–156.

102   "The Hon. Thaddeus...saw in my life" Carpenter, *Six Months at the White House*, 173–174.

104   "Suddenly, the door...to be exchanged" Bullock, "President Lincoln's Visiting-Card," 567–569.

107   "A widow and...at the front" Wilson, *Intimate Memories of Lincoln*, 572–573.

110   "Exactly how long...in the pillows and cried" Wilson, *Intimate Memories of Lincoln*, 555–556.

CHAPTER 5

115   "for such a man" Greiner, Coryell, and Smither, *A Surgeon's Civil War*, 220.

116   "to suit the soldiers" Gaff, *On Many a Bloody Field*, 197.

116   "battles of his country" Basler, *Collected Works*, 7:395.

116   "due to the soldier" Basler, *Collected Works*, 7:253–254.

117   "prosperity of this country" Basler, *Collected Works*, 5:438.

117   "customary in Europe" Basler, *Collected Works*, 5:354.

118   "quickly won their trust" Burlingame, *Abraham Lincoln: Observations*, 71.

119   "met him on all sides" Porter, *Campaigning with Grant*, 275.

119   "length of the lines" Davis, *Lincoln's Men*, 141.

120   "his shaggy eyebrows" Davis, *Lincoln's Men*, 141.

120   "old man's mind" Carter, *Four Brothers in Blue*, 235.

120   "kindly face grew deeper" Stevens, *As If It Were Glory*, 13.

120 "must be very great" Greiner, Coryell, and Smither, *A Surgeon's Civil War*, 87.

120 "to the echo" Fuller, *Personal Recollections*, 46.

120 "in his palmist days" Davis, *Lincoln's Men*, 68.

121 "see and salute him" Burlingame, *Abraham Lincoln: A Life*, 2:425.

121 "trusted him—was true" Jones, *Four Years*, 208.

121 "as a major general" Wilson, *Intimate Memories of Lincoln*, 498.

122 "Mr. Lincoln's...the American soldier" Brooks, *Washington in Lincoln's Time*, 77–78.

124 "My first view...glad I enlisted" Wilson, *Intimate Memories of Lincoln*, 485.

125 "A very handsome...faithful to his duty" Rice, *Reminiscences of Abraham Lincoln*, 242–244.

128 "The President...of the land" Carpenter, *Six Months at the White House*, 170.

129 "I was detailed...upon full pay" Ward, *Abraham Lincoln: Tributes*, 191–192.

131 "He came often...with his presence" Stearns, *Lady Nurse of Ward E*, 8, 42.

132 "In my daily...his own family" Doster, *Lincoln and Episodes of the Civil War*, 24.

133 "Passing through...the latter's recovery" Segal, *Conversations with Lincoln*, 210.

135   "Just as they...the dying boy" Wilson, *Intimate Memories of Lincoln*, 435–436.

136   "The surgeon asked...home in Washington" Carpenter, *Six Months at the White House*, 287.

POSTSCRIPT

143   "a happier and better man" Speed, *Reminiscences of Abraham Lincoln*, 32–33.

143   "could not give him" Burlingame, *Lincoln Observed*, 194.

143   "His own purposes" Basler, *Collected Works*, 8:333.

143   "with all nations" Basler, *Collected Works*, 8:333.

144   "One morning... Low for me" Carter, *She Knew Lincoln*, 6–20.

BIBLIOGRAPHY

Basler, Roy P., ed., Marion Dolores Pratt and Lloyd A. Dunlap, asst. eds. *The Collected Works of Abraham Lincoln*. New Brunswick, NJ: Rutgers University Press, 1955.

Bates, Homer. *Lincoln in the Telegraph Office: Recollections of the United States Military Telegraph Corps during the Civil War*. New York: Century, 1907.

Brooks, Noah. *Washington in Lincoln's Time*. New York: Century, 1895.

Browne, Francis F. *The Every-day Life of Abraham Lincoln: A Narrative And Descriptive Biography With Pen-Pictures And Personal Recollections By Those Who Knew Him*. Chicago: Browne & Howell Company, 1913.

Bullock, John M. "President Lincoln's Visiting-Card: The Story of the Parole of a Confederate Officer." *The Century Magazine* 55, no. 4 (Feb. 1898): 565–572.

Burlingame, Michael. *Abraham Lincoln: A Life*. Baltimore: Johns Hopkins University Press, 2008.

————, ed. *Abraham Lincoln: The Observations of John G. Nicolay and John Hay*. Carbondale: Southern Illinois University Press, 2007.

————, ed. *At Lincoln's Side: John Hay's Civil War Correspondence and Selected Writings*. Carbondale: Southern Illinois University Press, 2000.

————. *The Inner World of Abraham Lincoln*. Urbana: University of Illinois Press, 1994.

————. *An Oral History of Abraham Lincoln: John G. Nicolay's Interviews and Essays*. Carbondale: Southern Illinois University Press, 1996.

Carpenter, F. B. *The Inner Life of Abraham Lincoln*. Boston: Houghton, Mifflin & Co., 1883.

————. *Six Months at the White House with Abraham Lincoln: The Story of a Picture*. New York: Hurd and Houghton, 1866.

Carter, Esther May. *She Knew Lincoln*. Cuyahoga Falls, OH: Esther May Carter, 1930.

Carter, Robert Goldthwaite. *Four Brothers in Blue: A Story of the Great Civil War from Bull Run to Appomattox*. Washington, DC: Gibson Brothers, 1913.

Carwardine, Richard J. *Lincoln: Profiles in Power*. New York: Knopf, 2006.

Colfax, Schuyler. *The Life and Principles of Abraham Lincoln*. Philadelphia: James B. Rodgers, 1865.

BIBLIOGRAPHY

Davis, William C. *Lincoln's Men: How President Lincoln Became a Father to an Army and a Nation*. New York: Free Press, 1999.

Donald, David H. *Lincoln*. New York: Touchstone, 1996.

Doster, William E. *Lincoln and Episodes of the Civil War*. New York: G. P. Putnam's Sons, 1915.

Douglass, Frederick. *The Life and Times of Frederick Douglass, Written by Himself*. London: Christian Age Office, 1882.

Fehrenbacher, Don E., and Virginia Fehrenbacher. *Recollected Words of Abraham Lincoln*. Stanford, CA: Stanford University Press, 1996.

Fuller, Charles A. *Personal Recollections of the War of 1861 as Private, Sargeant, and Lieutenant in the Sixty-First Regiment, New York Volunteer Infantry*. New York: News Job Printing, 1906.

Gaff, Alan D. *On Many a Bloody Field: Four Years in the Iron Brigade*. Indianapolis: Indiana University Press, 1996.

Gienapp, William E. *Abraham Lincoln and Civil War America*. New York: Oxford University Press, 2002.

Greiner, J. M., J. L. Coryell, and J. R. Smither, eds. *A Surgeon's Civil War: The Letters and Diaries of Daniel M. Holt, M.D.* Kent, OH: Kent State University Press, 1994.

Harris, William C. *Lincoln and the Border States: Preserving the Union*. Lawrence: University Press of Kansas, 2011.

Herndon, William H., and Jesse K. Weik. *Herndon's Lincoln: The True Story of a Great Life*. Chicago: Belford–Clarke Company, 1889.

Hertz, Emanuel. *The Hidden Lincoln: From the Letters and Papers of William H. Herndon*. New York: Viking Press, 1938.

———. *Lincoln Talks: An Oral History of Abraham Lincoln*. New York: Viking Press, 1939.

Holzer, Harold. *Dear Mr. Lincoln: Letters to the President*. Carbondale: Southern Illinois University Press, 1993.

———. *Lincoln as I Knew Him: Gossip, Tributes, and Revelations from His Best Friends and Worst Enemies*. First paperback edition, 2009. Chapel Hill, NC: Algonquin Books, 1999.

Hubbard, Charles M. *Lincoln Reshapes the Presidency*. Macon, GA: Mercer University Press, 2003.

Jayne, William. *Personal Reminiscences of the Martyred President*. Chicago: Grand Army Hall and Memorial Association, 1908.

Jones, E. R. *Four Years in the Army of the Potomac: A Soldiers' Recollections*. London: Tyne Publishing Company, 1881.

Lamon, Ward Hill. *The Life of Abraham Lincoln: From His Birth to His Inauguration as President*. Boston: James R. Osgood and Company, 1872.

Lamon, Ward Hill. *Recollections of Abraham Lincoln 1847–1865*. Edited by Dorothy Lamon. Chicago: A. C. McClurg and Co., 1895.

McClure, Alexander K. *"Abe" Lincoln's Yarns and Stories*. Philadelphia: Winston, 1901.

Miers, Earl Schenk, ed. *Lincoln Day by Day: A Chronology, 1809–1865*. Washington, DC: Lincoln Sesquicentennial Commission, 1960.

BIBLIOGRAPHY

Mitgang, Herbert, ed. *Spectator of America: A Classic Document About Lincoln and Civil War America by a Contemporary English Correspondent, Edward Dicey*. Athens: University of Georgia Press, 1989.

Neill, Edward Duffield. *Reminiscences of the Last Year of President Lincoln's Life*. St. Paul, MN: Pioneer Press Co., 1885.

Nevins, Allan, ed. *Diary of the Civil War, 1860–1865: George Templeton Strong*. New York: Macmillan, 1952.

Nicolay, Helen. *Personal Traits of Abraham Lincoln*. New York: Century, 1913.

Nicolay, John G., and John Hay, eds. *Complete Works of Lincoln*. New York: Francis D. Tandy, 1905.

Nofi, Albert A. *A Civil War Treasury*. New York: Da Capo Press, 1995.

Oldroyd, Osborn H. *The Lincoln Memorial: Album-immortelles*. New York: G. W. Carleton & Company, 1882.

Phillips, Isaac N., ed. *Abraham Lincoln by Some Men Who Knew Him*. Bloomington, IL: Pantagraph Printing, 1910.

Porter, Horace. *Campaigning with Grant*. New York: Century, 1897.

Rice, Allen T. *Reminiscences of Abraham Lincoln by Distinguished Men of His Time*. New York: North American Review, 1888.

Roberts, Octavia. *Lincoln in Illinois*. Boston: Houghton, Mifflin & Co., 1918.

Russell, William Howard. *My Diary North and South*. London: Bradley and Evans, 1863.

Schurz, Carl. *Abraham Lincoln: An Essay*. Boston: Houghton, Mifflin & Co., 1891.

———. *Reminiscences of Carl Schurz*. New York: McClure, 1907.

Scripps, John Locke. *The First Published Life of Abraham Lincoln*. 1860. Reprint, Detroit, MI: Cranbrook Press, 1900.

Segal, Charles M. *Conversations with Lincoln*. New York: G. P. Putnam's Sons, 1961.

Speed, Joshua Fry. *Reminiscences of Abraham Lincoln and Notes of a Visit to California*. Louisville, KY: John P. Morgan and Company, 1884.

Stanton, Robert Brewster. "Abraham Lincoln: Personal Memories of the Man." *Scribner's Illustrated Magazine* LXVIII (July 1920): 32–41.

Stearns, Amanda Akin. *The Lady Nurse of Ward E*. New York: Baker & Taylor, 1909.

Stevens, Michael E., ed. *As If It Were Glory: Robert Beecham's Civil War from the Iron Brigade to the Black Regiments*. Lanham, MD: Rowman and Littlefield, 2007.

Stevens, Walter. *A Reporter's Lincoln*. St. Louis: Missouri Historical Society, 1916.

Stimmel, Smith. *Personal Reminiscences of Abraham Lincoln*. Minneapolis: William H. Adams, 1928.

Stoddard, William O. *Inside the White House in War Times*. New York: Charles L. Webster, 1892.

BIBLIOGRAPHY

Temple, Wayne C. *Abraham Lincoln: From Skeptic to Prophet*. Mahomet, IL: Mayhaven, 1995.

Thayer, William Roscoe. *The Life and Letters of John Hay*. Boston: Houghton, Mifflin & Co., 1915.

Thomas, Benjamin P. *Abraham Lincoln*. New York: Alfred Knopf, 1952.

Villard, Henry. *Memoirs of Henry Villard: Journalist and Financier, in Two Volumes*. Boston: Houghton, Mifflin & Co., 1904.

Ward, William Hayes, ed. *Abraham Lincoln: Tributes from his Associates, Reminiscences of Soldiers, Statesmen and Citizens*. New York: T. Y. Crowell & Company, 1895.

Whipple, Wayne. *The Story Life of Abraham Lincoln: A Biography Composed of Five Hundred True Stories Told By Abraham Lincoln and His Friends*. Chicago: John C. Winston Company, 1908.

Whitney, Henry. *Life on the Circuit with Lincoln*. Boston: Estes and Lauriat, 1892.

Wilson, Douglas, and Rodney Davis, eds. *Herndon's Informants: Letters, Interviews, and Statements About Abraham Lincoln*. Urbana: University of Illinois Press, 1998.

Wilson, Douglas L. *Honor's Voice: The Transformation of Abraham Lincoln*. New York: Alfred A. Knopf, 1998.

Wilson, Rufus Rockwell. *Lincoln Among His Friends: A Sheaf of Intimate Memories*. Caldwell, ID: Caxton Printers, Ltd., 1942.

———. *Intimate Memories of Lincoln*. Elmira, NY: Primavera Press, 1945.

PHOTO CREDITS

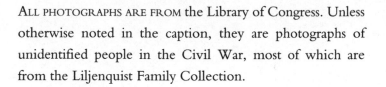

ALL PHOTOGRAPHS ARE FROM the Library of Congress. Unless otherwise noted in the caption, they are photographs of unidentified people in the Civil War, most of which are from the Liljenquist Family Collection.

INDEX

ABOUT THE AUTHOR

GORDON LEIDNER IS THE author of numerous books and articles about Abraham Lincoln and the American Civil War. A board member of the Abraham Lincoln Institute, he maintains the web-site GreatAmericanHistory.net, where he provides free educa-tional material to students and  educators on Abraham Lincoln, the Civil War, and the American Revolution.